TECH *Empowerment*™

Android App Inventor

A beginner's guide to Google Android App Inventor
by Eric Hamilton

Tech Empowerment: Android App Inventor

Published by

Lulu Press

3101 Hillsborough St

Raleigh, NC 27607

www.lulu.com

ISBN: 978-1-4583-7979-5

Manufactured in the United States of America

Content

About The Author

Eric Hamilton

New York, New York

Eric Hamilton is an internet, web, search marketing and social media veteran with over 20 years of technology work experience.

Eric has been designing Websites since 1994 and is the owner of Web Developers of New York, a Manhattan based web design firm. The firm prides itself on creating low cost high quality web solutions. The firm's client list includes NY Times bestselling author Zane, Ron Artest of the Los Angeles Lakers, Kalana Greene of the WNBA's New York Liberty and other clients. http://www.newyorkwideweb.com

Eric is the author of Social Media Branding in the Age of Obama, a social media guide. Eric frequently speaks at conferences and conventions on the topic of social media.

http://www.socialmediaobama.com

Eric founded The Web Academy, a 501c3 nonprofit organization designed to provide free web design classes to the community and low cost web services to non-profit organizations and low income businesses. As of early 2011, the Web Academy has had over 3000 enrollments. A percentage of the proceeds of this book will be donated to The Web Academy.

http://www.thewebacademy.org

Eric is from Detroit, Michigan, has a BS in Computer Science from Michigan State University, has been a proud member of Alpha Phi Alpha fraternity for more than 20 years and is active in the community with local high school science fairs as a Computer Science judge.

Acknowledgements

Mr. Dennis J. Keeney

I want to dedicate this book to my high school track/cross country coach, chemistry teacher and mentor, Mr. Dennis Keeney. In 1983, I was a freshman at Walled Lake Western high school. I was a cross country/track athlete and chemistry student of Mr. Keeney for most of my high school years. Mr. Keeney was NOT the usual 80's chemistry teacher/track coach. Mr. Keeney used cutting edge technology in his classroom and on the track.

The Classroom

One day in class, Mr. Keeney connected a computer to one of the school's TV monitors. Then he used a high tech input device called a Koala Pad to graphically demonstrate chemical bonds and other laws of chemistry.

Koala Pad by Koala Technologies (1984)

The Track

On the track, Mr. Keeney used hand held computers which looked like super bulky Blackberry devices. He used these devices to monitor and measure his athletes' performance times. Mr. Keeney could even print directly from these devices to a hand held printer.

In 1985, Mr. Keeney used the latest technology to help his students. It is with similar passion and dedication that I write this publication. It is my hope that I can positively inspire others as Mr. Keeney has positively inspired me.

About Mr. Dennis J. Keeney

Mr. Dennis J. Keeney started his career in education in 1974 for Walled Lake Consolidated Schools.

In 1982, Mr. Keeney moved to Walled Lake Western High School for 12 years where he began teaching English and American Literature and transitioned to a focus in Chemistry. In addition to teaching, Mr. Keeney was the Track & Field coach at Walled Lake Junior High School from 1975-1976. In 1977, he became the assistant Track & Field coach at Walled Lake Western High School, overtaking the Head Track & Field coach position from 1983-1994. In addition to Track, Mr. Keeney coached the Walled Lake Western High School Cross-Country Team from 1983-1994.

After serving as an educator and coach for 20 years, Mr. Keeney took his passion to the next level and became the Math and Science Coordinator for the Walled Lake Consolidated Schools district from 1994-2004. In 2004, Mr. Keeney was appointed in an administrative position as Director of Student Services for two years, and then appointed as Director of Technology and Data Analysis from 2006-2010.

Mr. Keeney's passion for education, coaching and development yielded many rewards. In 1988, he coached the individual National Cross-Country and National Two Mile Champion. In the early 1990's, his Cross-Country teams were a formidable team in the area, winning the League Championship four years in a row and placing 2nd in 1990 and 1991 in the state of Michigan. Mr. Keeney has made an impact in the lives of each student and athlete that he has touched.

After an illustrious career, Mr. Keeney humbly retired in June 2010 after serving Walled Lake Consolidated Schools for 36 years. Mr. Keeney is happily married to his wife of 36 years and has two grown sons, one grandson and his beloved golden retriever.

A special thanks to Mr. Keeney's wife, Sally Keeney. She willingly opened her home to the cross country teams as we spent countless Sunday afternoons running the back trails of Walled Lake, MI and using their home as a pit stop. Another special thanks to Mr. Keeney's sons Trevor and Brandon. Thank you for sharing your dad with us. Trevor, thank you for taking the time to compose this biographical information on your dad.

As a 16 year old high school student, I could not fully appreciate the influence that Mr. Keeney had on me. As a 41 year old, it's good to know that I had possible people like Mr. Keeney to influence me in technology and in life.

Walled Lake Western Men's Cross Country 1986

1

About Google

Android App

Inventor

Google Labs

Google Labs is a division of Google which allows Google Engineers to experiment with new thoughts and new technology in their spare time. These Google Engineers develop these projects and rely on regular people in the outside world to give feedback. The success of projects in Google Labs is dependent on acceptance by people like you and me. There is no guarantee that projects developed in Google Labs will become the next Gmail or Google Search. [1]

Google Android App Inventor

Google App Inventor is a Google Labs project and it is based heavily on research in educational computing. Specifically, App Inventor uses the block editor technology which is based on the Open Block Java Library which is used in creating visual blocks programming languages. Open Blocks is distributed by the Massachusetts Institute of Technology's Scheller Teacher Education Program and is based on thesis research by Ricarose Roque. In simple terms, Open Blocks uses a drag and drop interface to allow users to create applications. Google Android App Inventor is based on Open Blocks.[2]

With App Inventor you can create simple games, applications which access databases, applications that send text messages, applications that access web sites and applications that use GPS.[1]

Google Android App Inventor is changing the way software is developed. Traditionally, software development is achieved by programmers writing thousands of lines of cryptic source code. With Google App Inventor, non-software developers can use App Inventor's drag and drop technology to create applications that would otherwise take a software development expert to create.

Your 1st Mobile Applications

Have you ever wondered how and why software is always available for a hardware product when it hits the market? For instance, when the iPad first hit the market in early 2010, immediately there was available software by 3rd party providers. How are these 3rd party providers able to create software for a new product so quickly? Well, most of these providers were a part of the Apple's early developer program. They have access to Apple's SDKs (software development kit) and APIs (application programming interface) before the rest of the world.

During these early development stages, there are bugs that the 3rd party developers encounter that they would never encounter with a fully developed product. Well, if you are reading this book, then you are an early developer of Google App Inventor.

As of 2011, Google's App Inventor platform is in beta and has not been fully tested and debugged. If you are participating in an online class through the Web Academy, then your instructors are only a few months ahead of you. Patience and persistence are the keys success, so don't get upset if you have a difficult time just getting your development software to install properly. It will not always go as smoothly as you like and this is by design.

Certain buttons on your phone that need to be clicked will not be present. Device drivers will need to be downloaded from the manufacturer and installed and instructions for these tasks will NOT be in this publication or anywhere on the web. Your instructors and Google will not have all of the answers. If your instructors and Google cannot help you, then you must rely on user forums and searching the web for answers. If you are enrolled in the Web Academy, this course may be different from any other course that you have ever taken. If you are a Computer Science graduate (like myself) then this is par for the course and you know the routine so deal with it.

Web technology changes every 18 months. As an undergraduate Computer Science student in the late 80s and early 90s my programming courses were undefined in areas. Many times, my instructors were learning the material only months before the students.

When Things Don't Work Out As Planned

When you develop software applications, sometimes things don't work out like you plan from the start. This is especially true in a beta environment. When things fail, consider yourself lucky. During these failures you are presented with an opportunity to sharpen your troubleshooting skills and learn a few new things.

In the creation of this book, I spent a lot of time installing the device drivers that allow my laptop to communicate with my Droid phone. This process was a nightmare as my Motorola Droid phone is new on the market.

During my research I learned a few new things about Motorola's SDK (Software Development Kit). The Motorola SDK is not necessary for App Inventor but it was a great learning experience. Remember, you are an early adopter so road blocks are a part of the game so be patient and have some fun.

Computer

Programming

Before getting deep into App Inventor, I would like to do an overview of where we have been in regards to computers and programming.

The Abacus

One of the earliest "computers" was the abacus. The abacus is a simple counting device used to add, subtract, multiply and divide. [3]   One could consider the manipulation of the beads on the abacus a simple form of programming. See Figure 2.1.

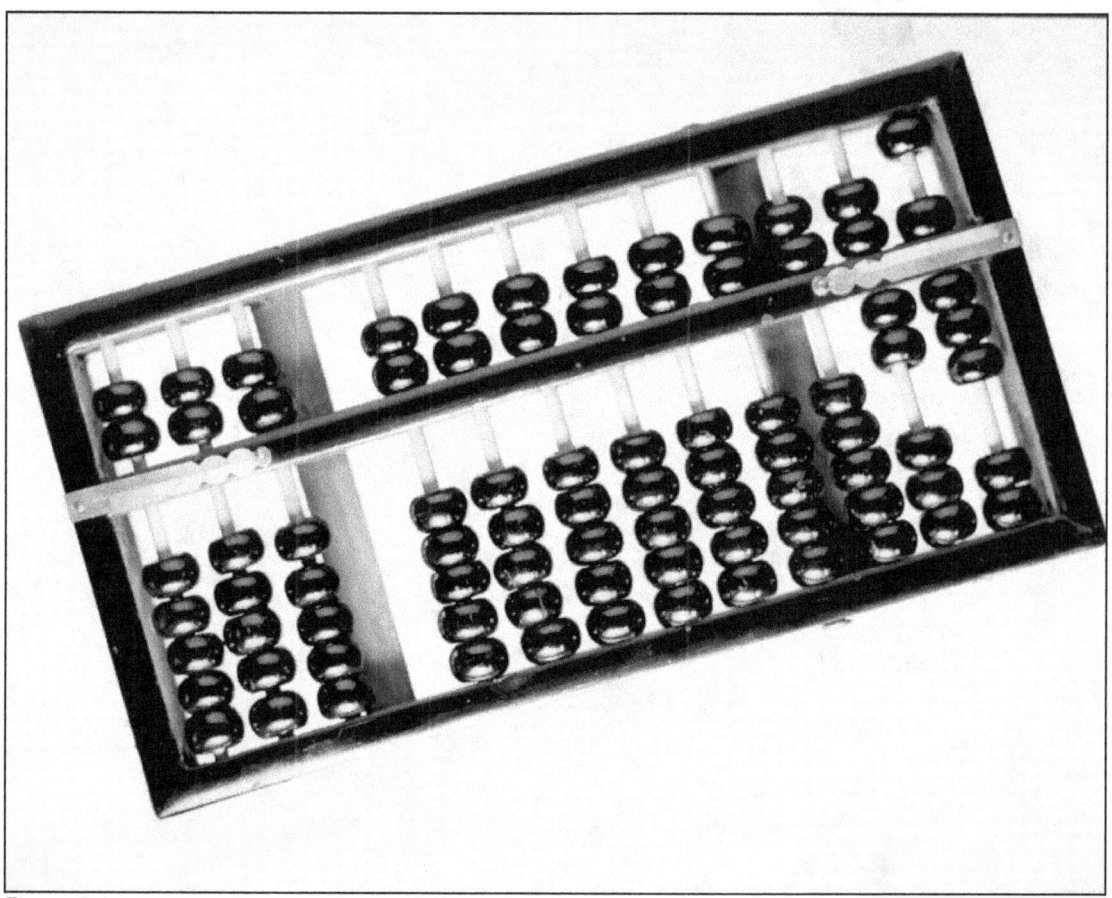

Figure 2.1

12

Analytical Machine

Charles Babbage was an English mathematician in the 1800s. Babbage's Analytical Machine was a mechanical general purpose computer which used punch cards as input. [4] See Figure 2.2.

Figure 2.2

The programming language used to program the Analytical Machine was similar to modern Assembly Language. Assembly Language is a low level computer programming language used to complete basic arithmetic computations such as storing values in variables. [5]

von Neumann Architecture

The von Neumann Architecture model (also known as the stored program computer) was the first to use a central processing unit (CPU) and stored memory. This model kept computer programs in RAM (random access memory) which allowed for fast access to the stored data. The control unit and arithmetic logic unit form the main components of the CPU.[6]   See Figure 2.3

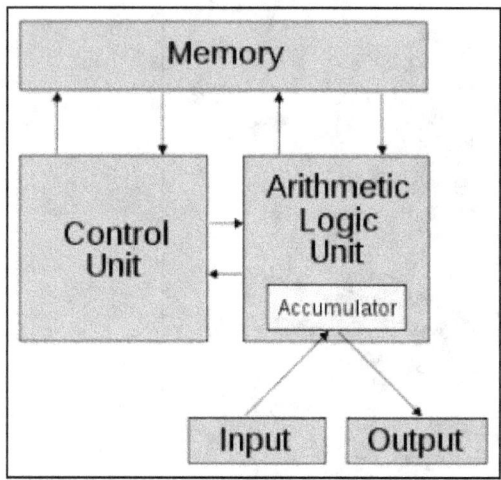

Figure 2.3

High Level Programming Languages

The computer language FORTRAN which stands for Formula Translation was one the first high level programming languages.   Instead of writing code in cryptic Assembly language, FORTRAN was more abstract and allowed the programmer to focus less on the details of the program. [7]

When I first learned to program, I used BASIC (Beginner's All-purpose Symbolic Instruction Code) on my Commodore 64 computer. BASIC was a high level programming language which simply executed the command lines of the program sequentially. See Figure 2.4

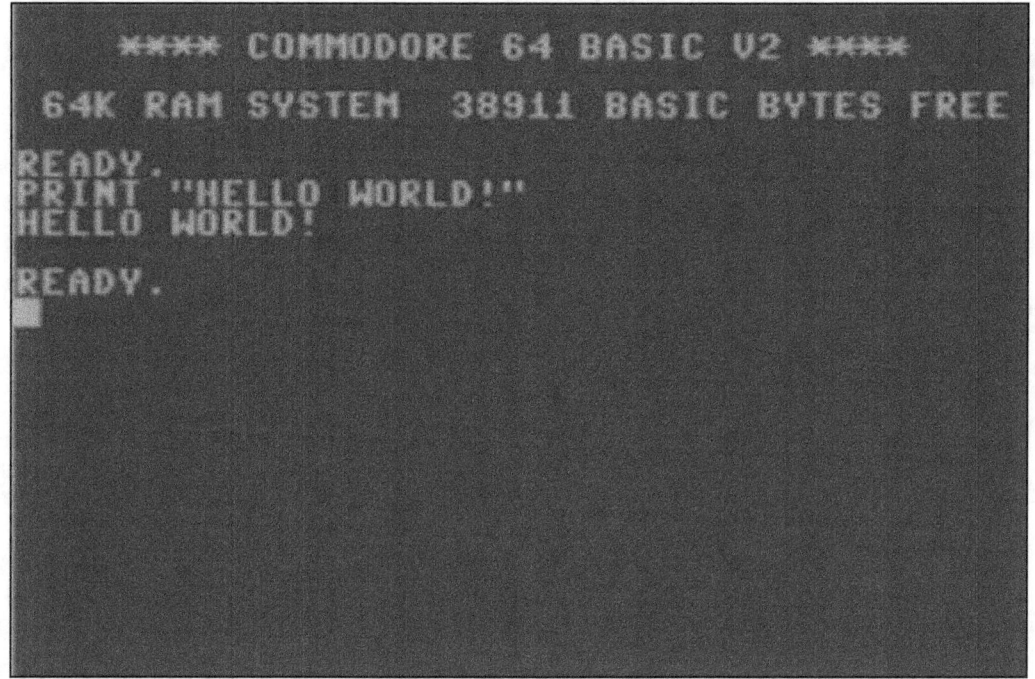

Figure 2.4

Object Oriented Programming

Object Oriented Programming is a programming concept that uses objects which are data structures. This methodology allows parts of the program to be stored as objects and called upon later when needed.

Mobile Application Development

Mobile application development is the process of developing applications on devices with limited memory and computing power. Mobile application development traditionally has been difficult because of the different mobile device hardware available and the different development platforms. As you know, in this book, we will focus solely on Android phones and we will be learning Google Android App Inventor. [8]

3

Setup Your Computer & Mobile Device

The first thing that we need to accomplish is to setup our computer. The instructions in this book mainly pertain to Windows. Below are the minimum system and web browser requirements for the Macintosh, Linux and Windows.

System Requirements

Computer and operating system:

* Macintosh (with Intel processor): Mac OS X 10.5, 10.6

* Windows: Windows XP, Windows Vista, Windows 7

* GNU/Linux: Ubuntu 8+, Debian 5+

Browser:

* Mozilla Firefox 3.6 or higher

* Apple Safari 5.0 or higher

* Google Chrome 4.0 or higher

* Microsoft Internet Explorer 7 or higher

Java Installation

After you have verified that the minimum system requirements have been met, you will need to download and install Java 6 (also known as Java 1.6). The Google Android App Inventor interface relies on Java to function.

Visit http://www.java.com and click "Free Java Download". See Figure 3.1.

Search
Java
Java in Action
Downloads
Help Center
JAVA + YOU,
DOWNLOAD
TODAY!
Free Java Download
» What is Java? » Do I have Java? » Need Help?
Experience Java in Action
Alice
Java + Alice
Java + Livescribe
Java + Neil Young
Java + Blu-ray Disc
Java + Mifos
Java + Amazon Kindle
Select Language | About Java | Partner with Us | Developers
Privacy | Terms of Use | Trademarks | Disclaimer
ORACLE

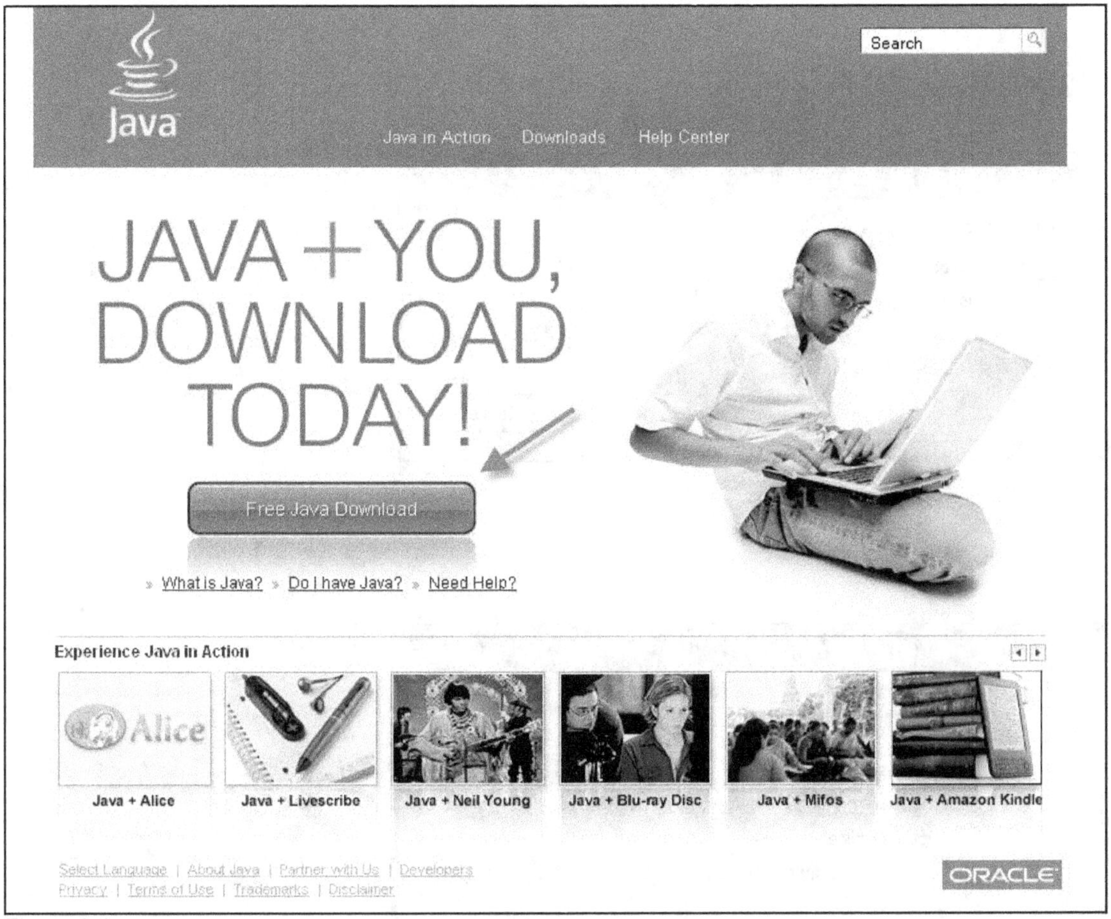

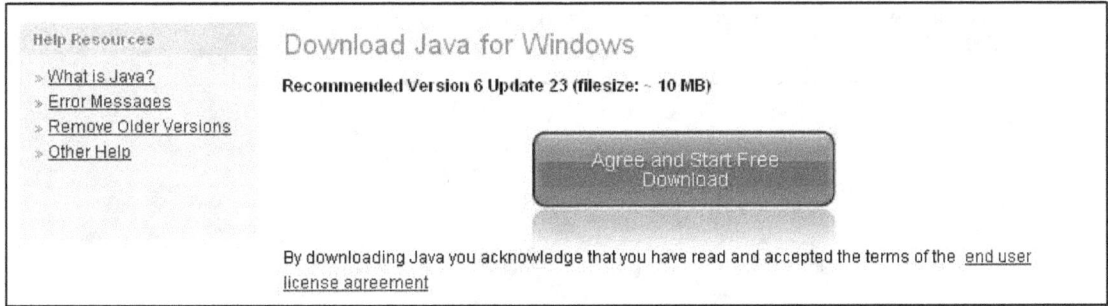

Figure 3.1

Next click "Agree and Start Free Download". See Figure 3.2.

Help Resources
» What is Java?
» Error Messages
» Remove Older Versions
» Other Help
Download Java for Windows
Recommended Version 6 Update 23 (filesize: ~ 10 MB)
Agree and Start Free Download
By downloading Java you acknowledge that you have read and accepted the terms of the end user license agreement

Figure 3.2

Next, save the .exe file and run that file. See Figure 3.3.

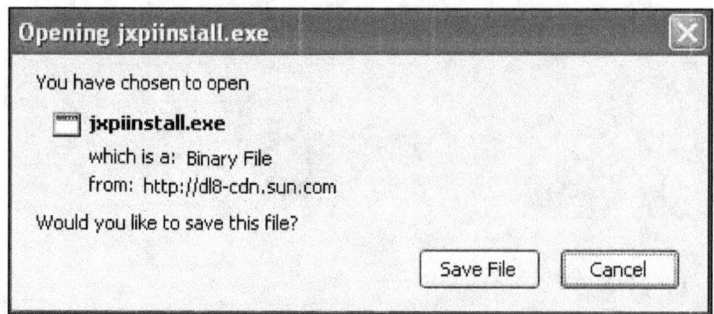

Figure 3.3

Next, click "Run". See Figure 3.4.

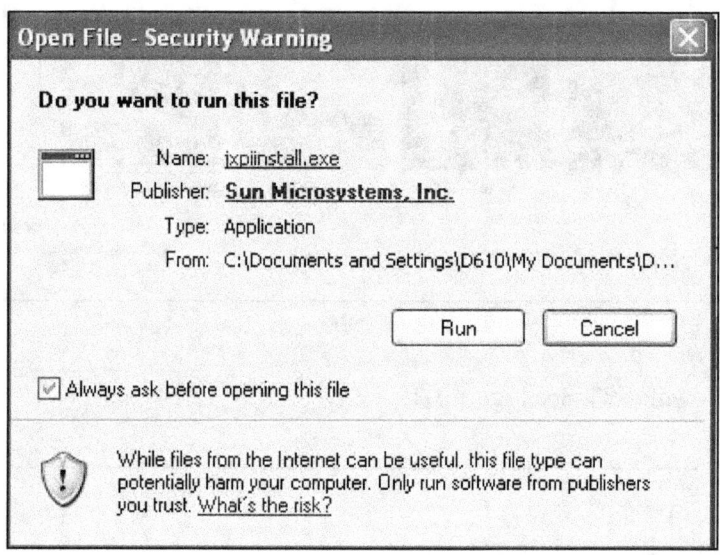

Figure 3.4

20

Next, you will see the Welcome screen, click Install. See Figure 3.5.

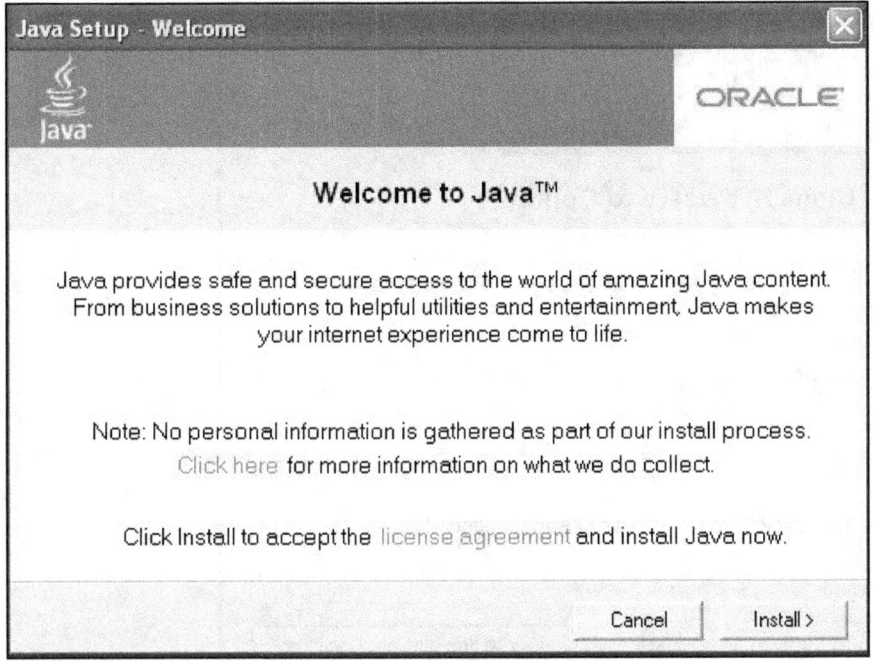

Figure 3.5

Next, the installer will download. See Figure 3.6.

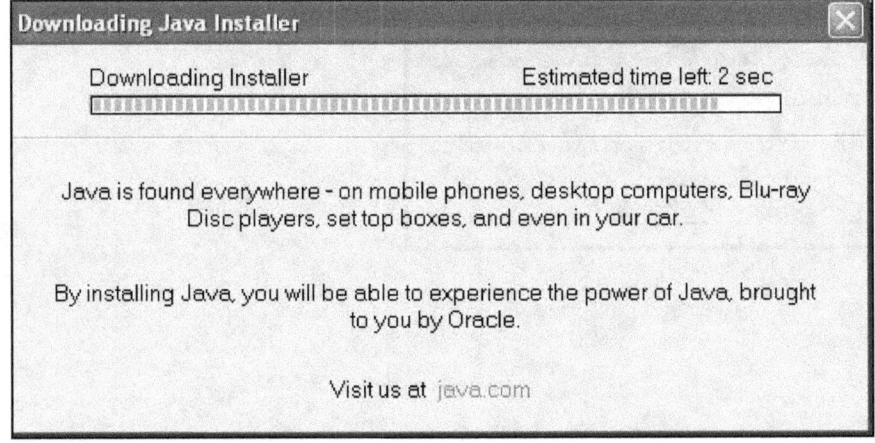

Figure 3.6

Next, the installation will need to close any browser windows that you have open. Click "Close

Browsers and Continue". See Figure 3.7.

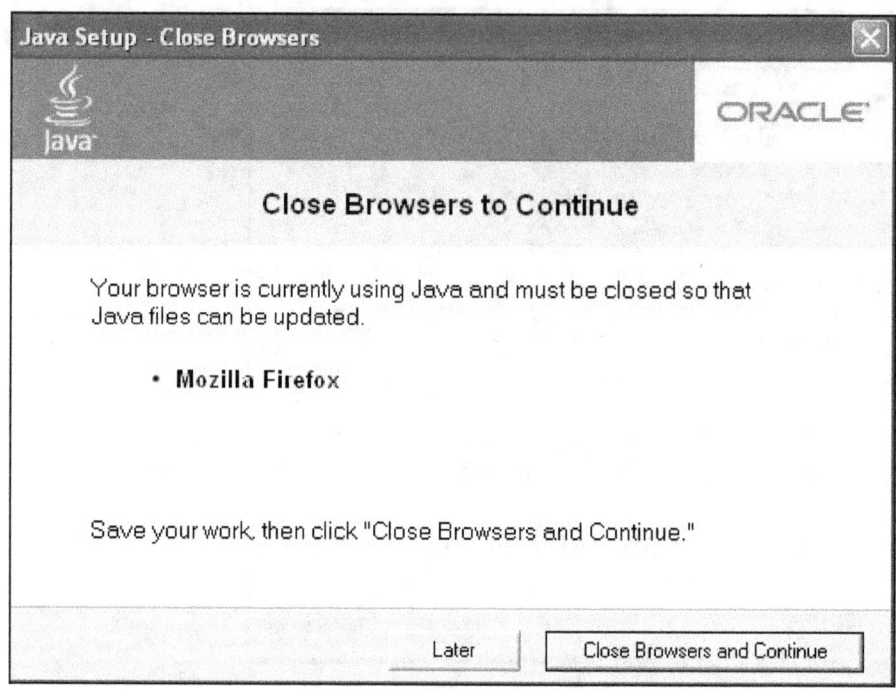

Figure 3.7

On the Close Browsers window, click OK. See Figure 3.8.

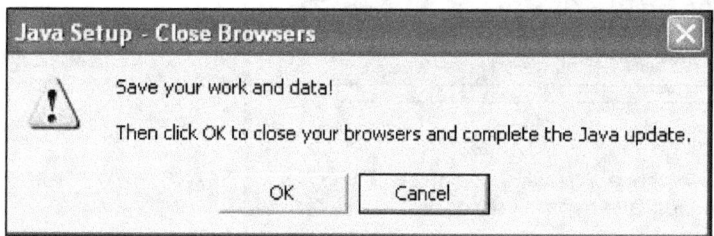

Figure 3.8

Next, Java will install. See Figure 3.9.

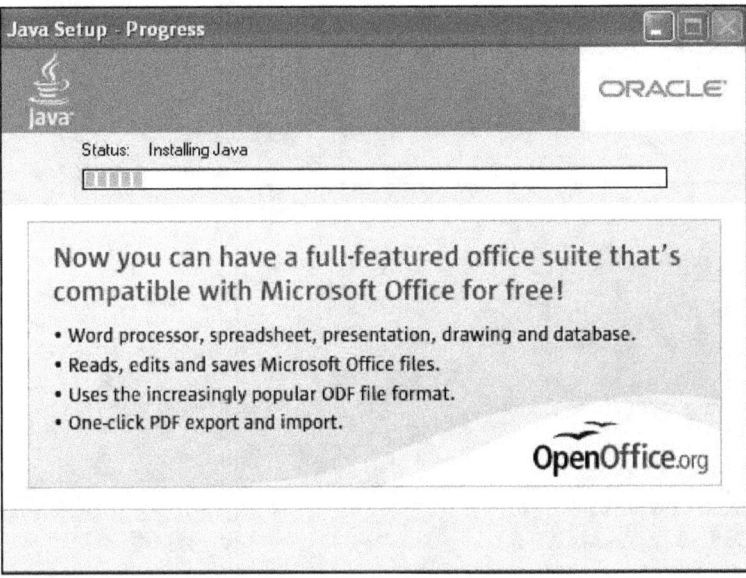

Figure 3.9

You will see "You have successfully installed Java", once the installation has completed successfully. See Figure 3.10.

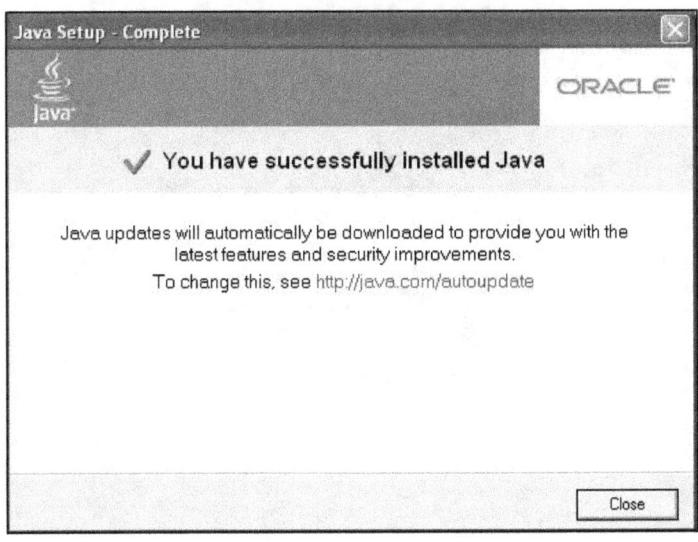

Figure 3.10

Test Java

To test your installation of Java, visit: http://www.java.com/en/download/help/testvm.xml .

If Java has been installed successfully, you will see the following confirmation message. See Figure 3.11.

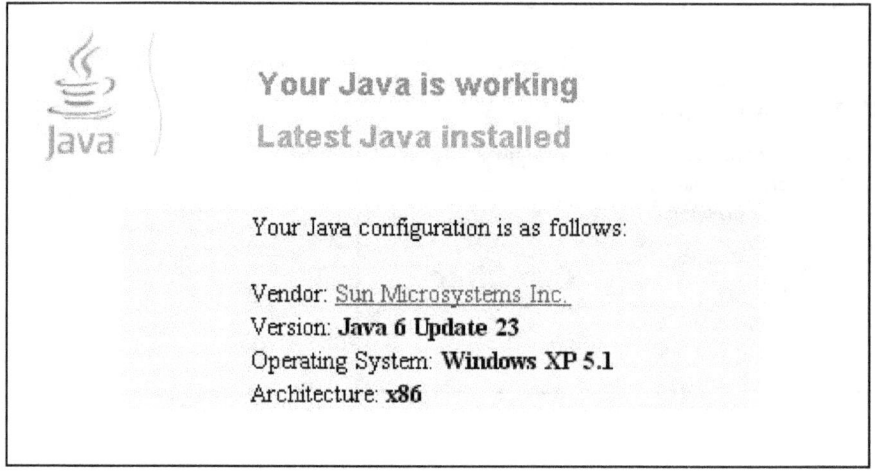

Figure 3.11

Next visit the Java Web Start Demos page at:

http://www.oracle.com/technetwork/java/demos-nojavascript-137100.html

Click the "Click to Launch!" icon. See Figure 3.12.

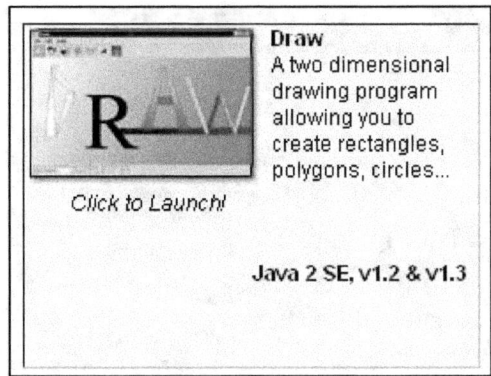

Figure 3.12

Next, click OK, to open and launch the application. See Figure 3.13.

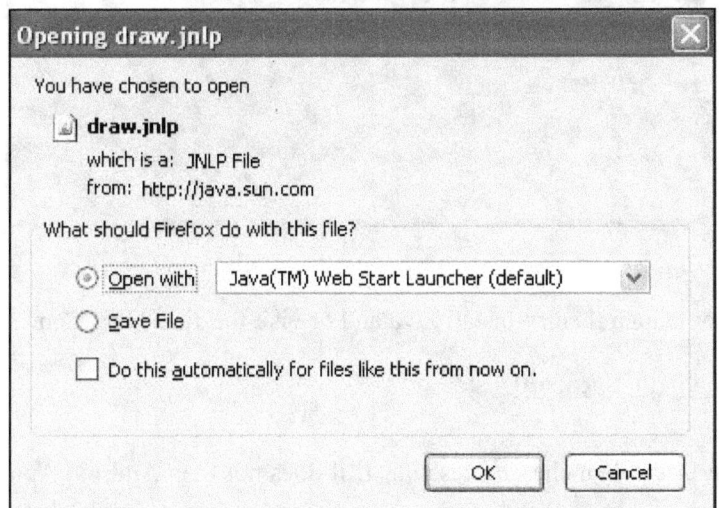

Figure 3.13

The Java Web Start Demo will launch. See Figure 3.14.

Figure 3.14

If the Java Web Start Demo does not launch then re-install Java and or visit the Java Help Center

at http://www.java.com/en/download/help/index.xml

It is crucial that the Java Web Start Demo launches successful. If it does not then Android App

Inventor will not work. Do not attempt to use Android App Inventor until the Java Web Start

Demo functions.

Install Android App Inventor

For Macintosh installations visit: http://appinventor.googlelabs.com/learn/setup/setupmac.html

For Linux installations visit: http://appinventor.googlelabs.com/learn/setup/setuplinux.html

The following instructions pertain to a Windows installation.

Visit http://appinventor.googlelabs.com/learn/setup/setupwindows.html and click Download. See Figure 3.15.

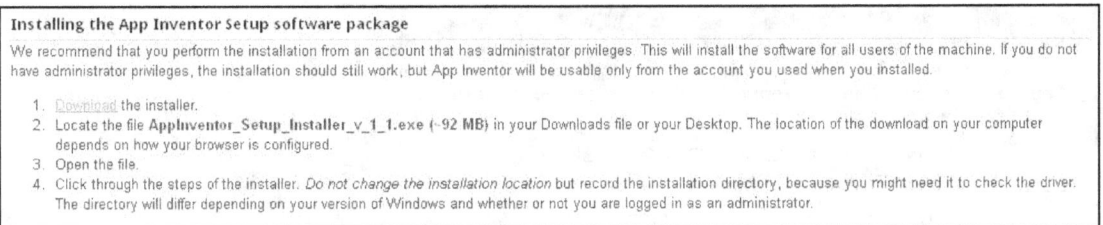

Figure 3.15

Click "Save File". See Figure 3.16.

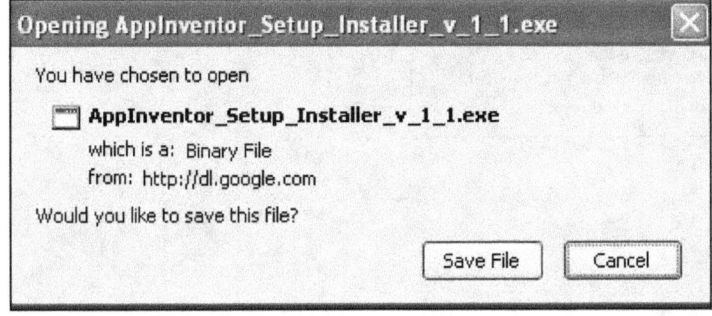

Figure 3.16

Next, locate your saved file and double click it. Click "OK" to run it. See Figure 3.17.

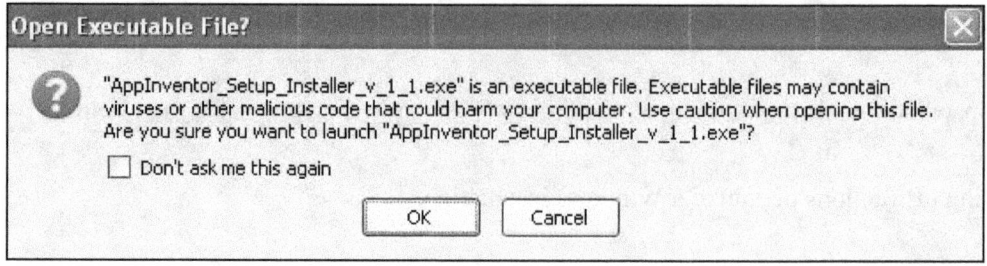

Figure 3.17

On the Security Warning screen, click Run. See Figure 3.18.

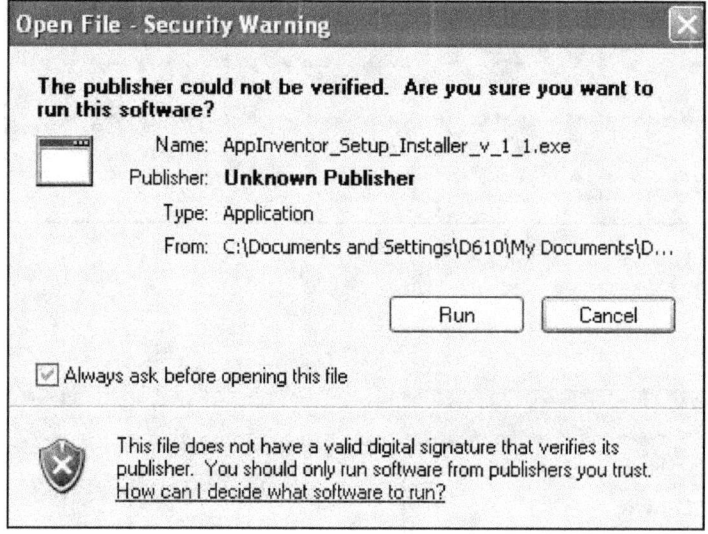

Figure 3.18

28

On the App Inventor Setup Wizard screen, click Next. See Figure 3.19.

Figure 3.19

On the App Inventor License Agreement screen, click "I Agree". See Figure 3.20.

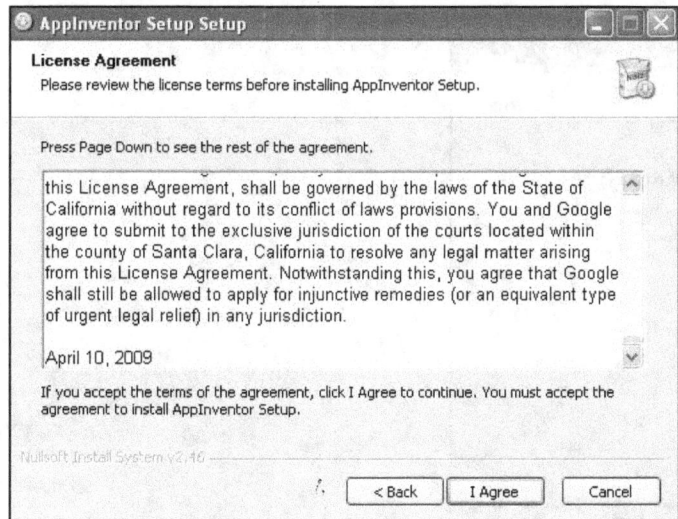

Figure 3.20

On the "Choose Install Location" screen, select the default destination folder and click Next.

See Figure 3.21.

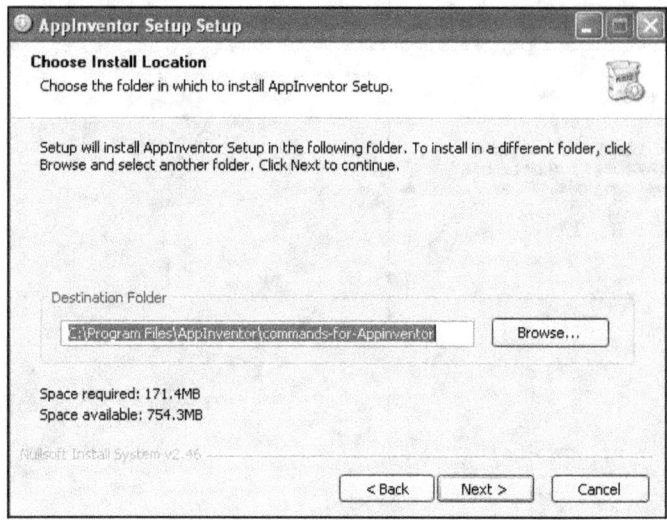

Figure 3.21

Next, select the default Start Menu folder (AppInventor Setup) and click Install. See Figure 3.22.

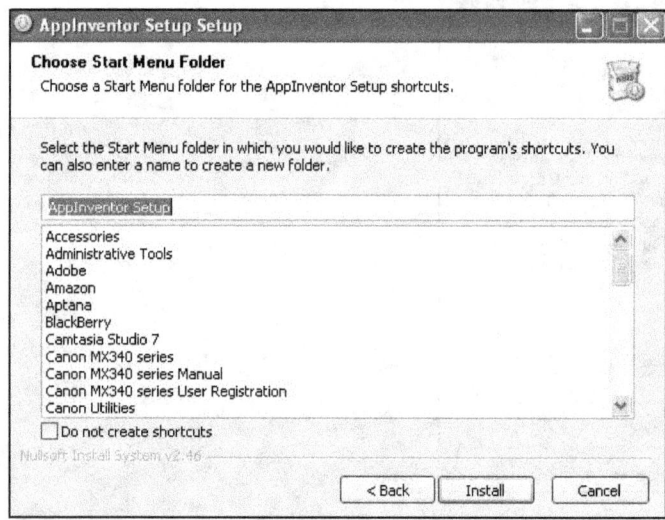

Figure 3.22

After the App Inventor installation has completed, click Finish. See Figure 3.23.

Figure 3.23

Locate Your Installation

The path of your installation of App Inventor should be C:\Program Files\AppInventor\commands-for-Appinventor\

See Figure 3.24.

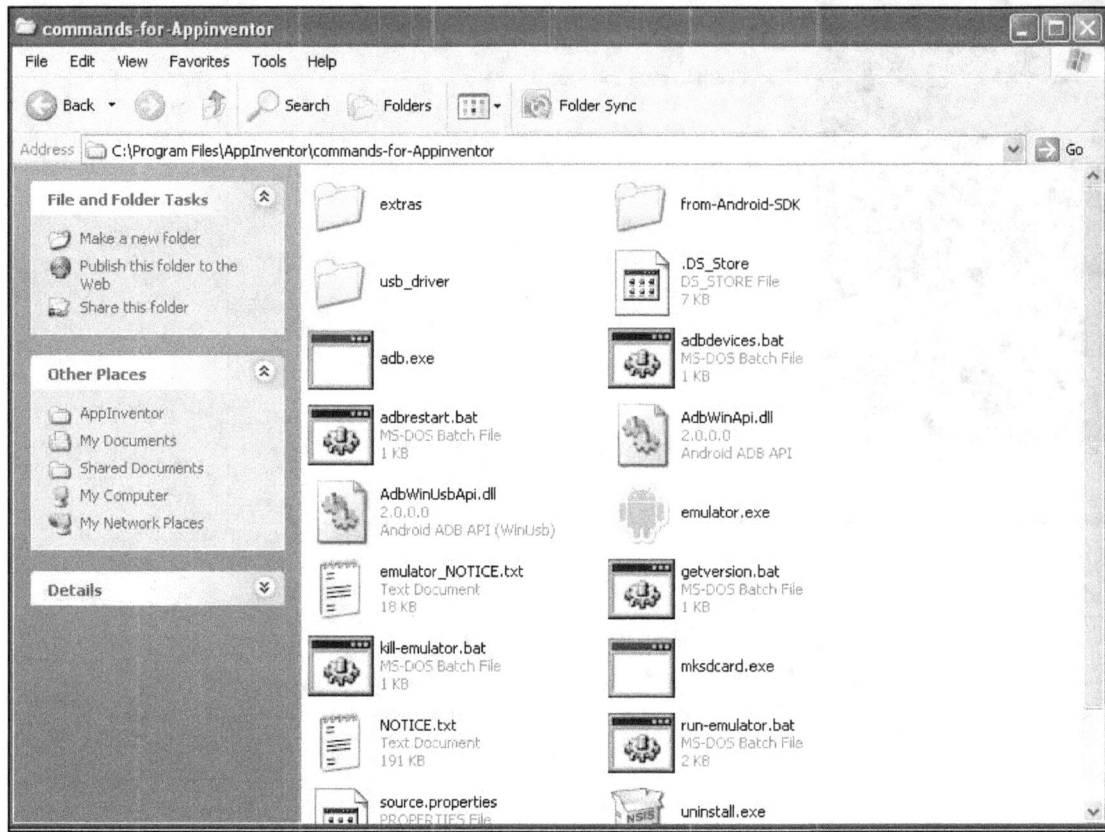

Figure 3.24

If your installation is not located at C:\Program Files\AppInventor\commands-for-Appinventor\

Then you can locate it by searching for the folder "commands-for-Appinventor".

To locate your installation click Start. See Figure 3.25

Figure 3.25

Next, click Search. See Figure 3.26.

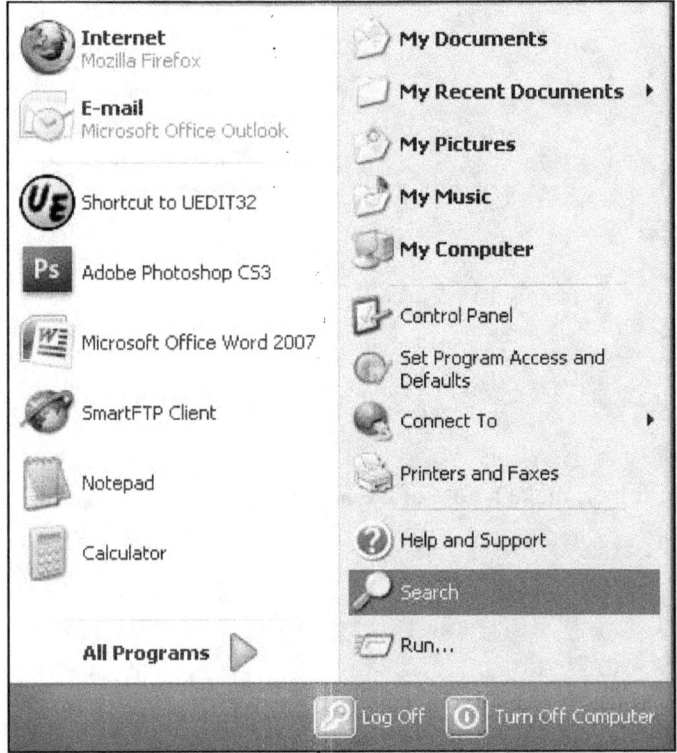

Figure 3.26

Next, search for "commands-for-Appinventor". See Figure 3.27

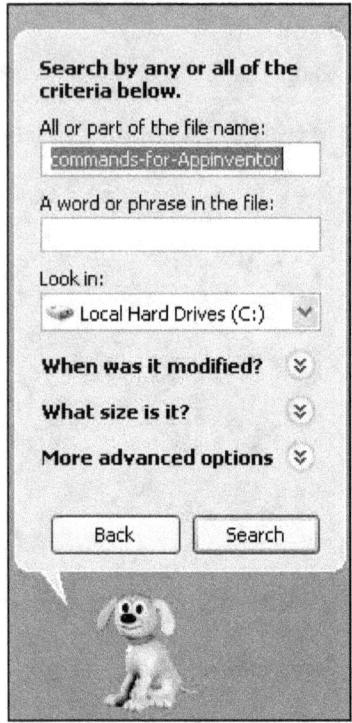

Figure 3.27

Once Windows locates your installation folder, make a note of the location.

Phone Drivers

A device driver (phone driver) is simply software that allows your computer to communicate with external hardware. Your computer will need to communicate directly with your Android phone, thus device drivers will need to be installed on your computer. The phone driver installation is the most tricky part of the installation process because each phone model is different with potentially different driver requirements.

According to Google Labs, the App Inventor Setup software includes drivers for these common Android phones:

- T-Mobile G1 / ADP1

- T-Mobile myTouch 3G* / Google Ion / ADP2

- Verizon Droid

- Nexus One

Next, we will check to see if App Inventor installed the drivers for your phone. We can do this by following the procedures below.

On your Windows PC, click Start. See Figure 3.29.

Figure 3.29

Next click Run. See Figure 3.30.

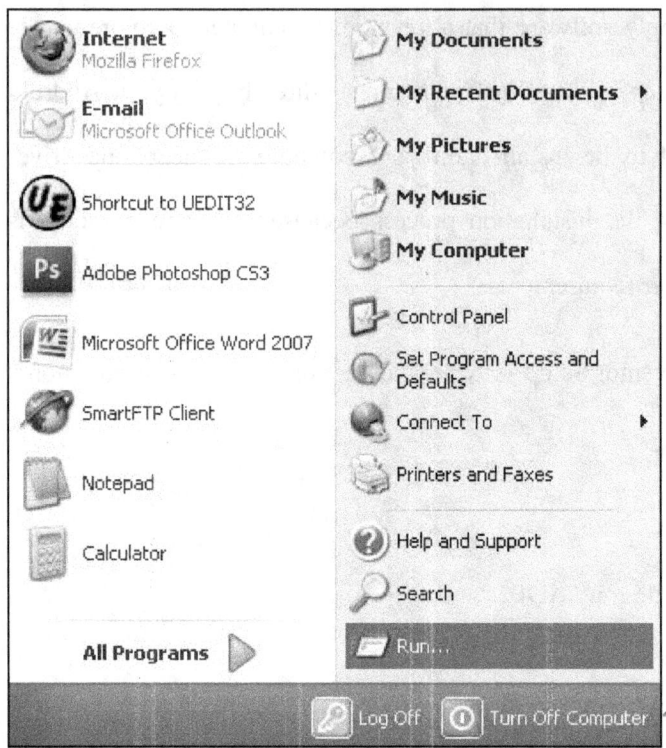

Figure 3.30

Next type "CMD" and click OK. See Figure 3.31.

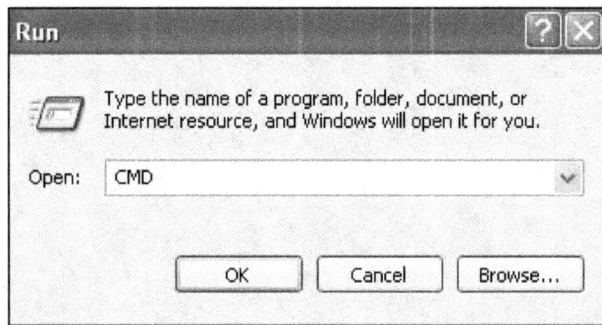

Figure 3.31

Next, you will need to change directory to the location of your App Inventor Installation. My installation location is at c:\Program Files\AppInventor\commands-for-Appinventor so I type: "cd c:\Program Files\AppInventor\commands-for-Appinventor" and hit Enter. CD means change directory. See Figure 3.32.

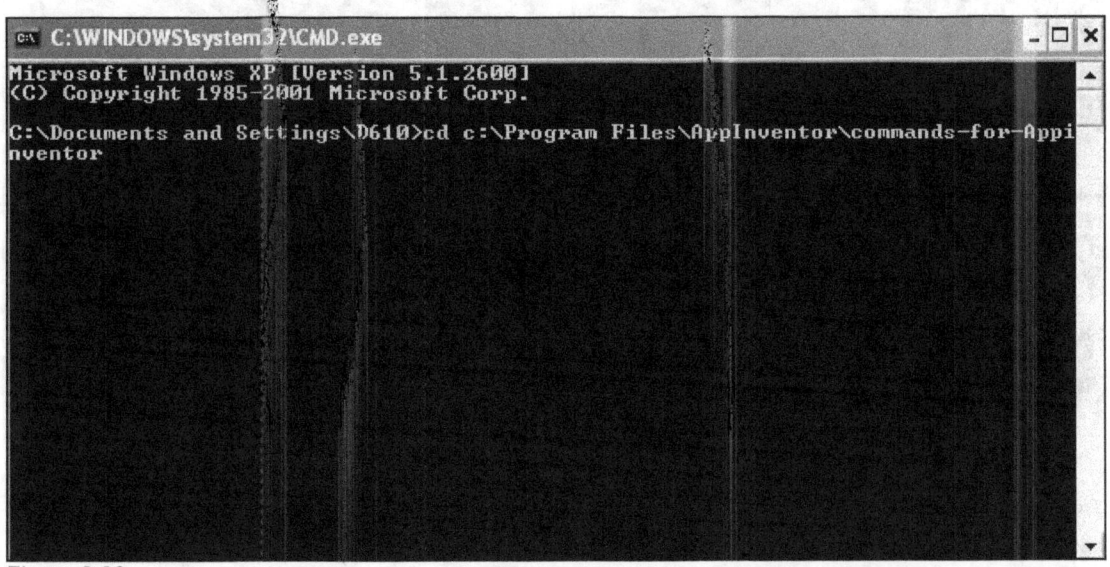

Figure 3.32

Next, I want to see the contents of the director so I type "dir" and hit Enter. See Figure 3.33.

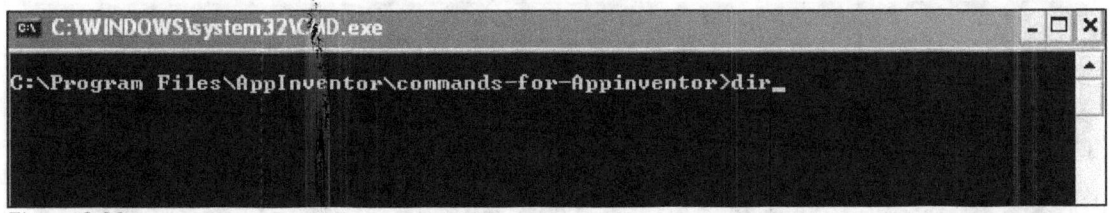

Figure 3.33

Notice the abd.exe file. This file is that we will use to determine if our device drivers have been

loaded. See Figure 3.34.

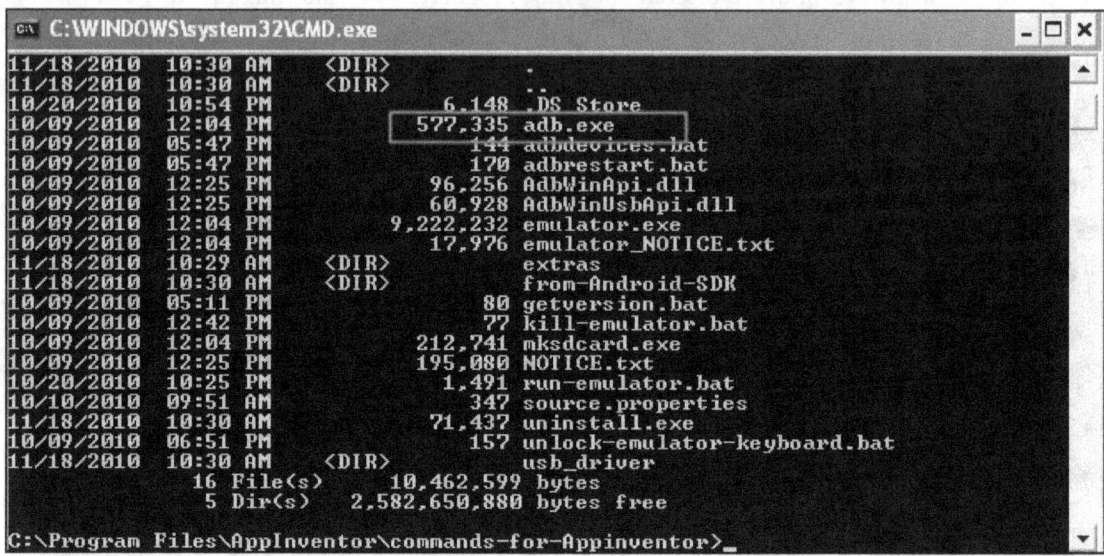

Figure 3.34

Next, <u>connect your phone to your PC with your USB cable</u> and type "adb devices". See Figure

3.35

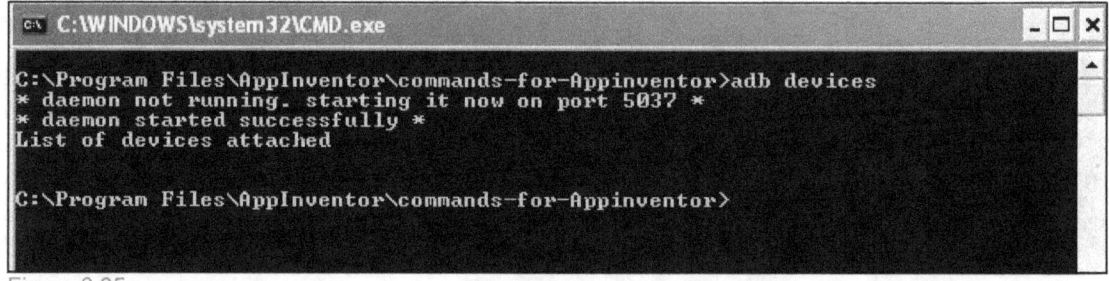

Figure 3.35

Notice that the list of devices attached is empty. This means that no drivers are installed or no

phone is attached to your PC. App Inventor did NOT install drivers for my Verizon Droid 2

even though Google Labs said that the drivers should be installed. Because App Inventor is in

Beta, you may experience similar setbacks. Because no phone drivers were found, we need to download and install them.

PDANet is a phone driver that I recommend. You can download it from the software manufacturer June Fabrics (an unusual name for a software manufacturer) at http://www.junefabrics.com/android/download.php

You can also download it from the web site for this publication. I prefer to download it from the web site for this publication so I visit:

http://android-apps-development.com/home/android-phone-driver-download/

See Figure 3.36.

Figure 3.36

Next, I click PDANet Version 2.45 installer for 32-bit Windows 7/Vista/XP. If you don't know whether to select the 32-bit version or the 64-bit version, then select the 32-bit version.

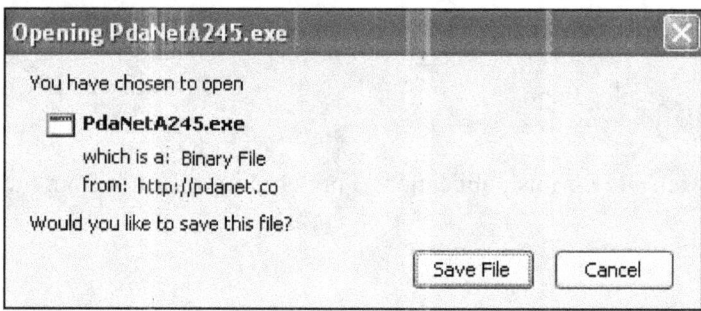

Figure 3.37

Next, save the file called PdaNetA245.exe. Next, open and install this file and select all of the defaults.

Next, if you removed the USB connection then re-connect your phone to your PC and repeat the steps to verify the driver installation as follows:

Click Start. See Figure 3.38

Figure 3.38

Next click Run. See Figure 3.39.

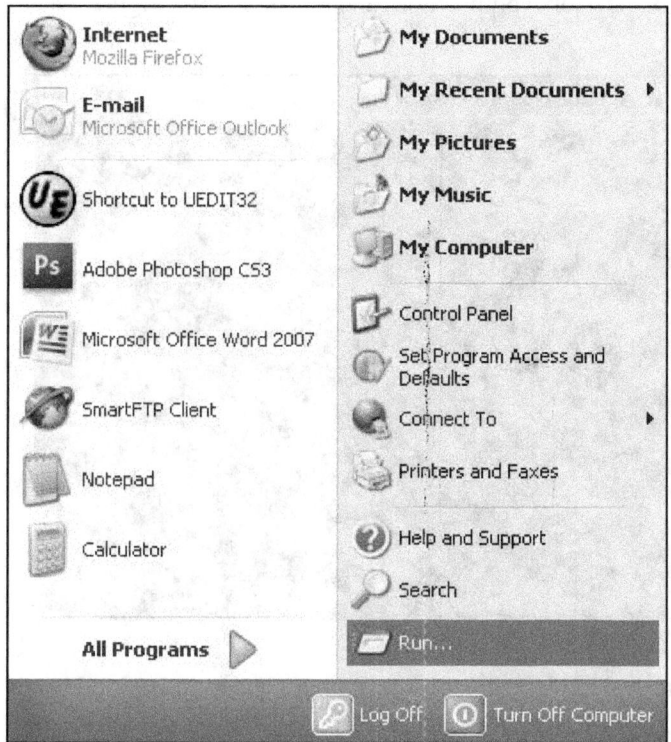

Figure 3.39

Next type "CMD" and click OK. See Figure 3.40.

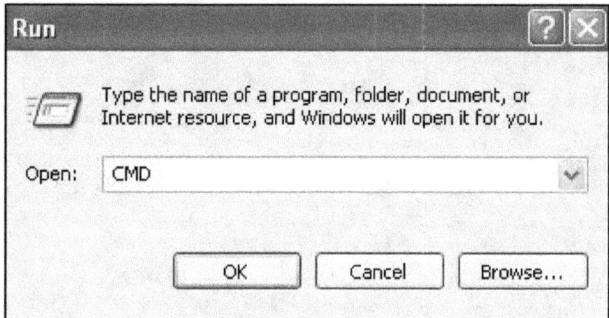

Figure 3.40

41

Next you will need to change directory to the location of your App Inventor Installation. My installation location is at c:\Program Files\AppInventor\commands-for-Appinventor so I type: "cd c:\Program Files\AppInventor\commands-for-Appinventor" and hit Enter. See Figure 3.41.

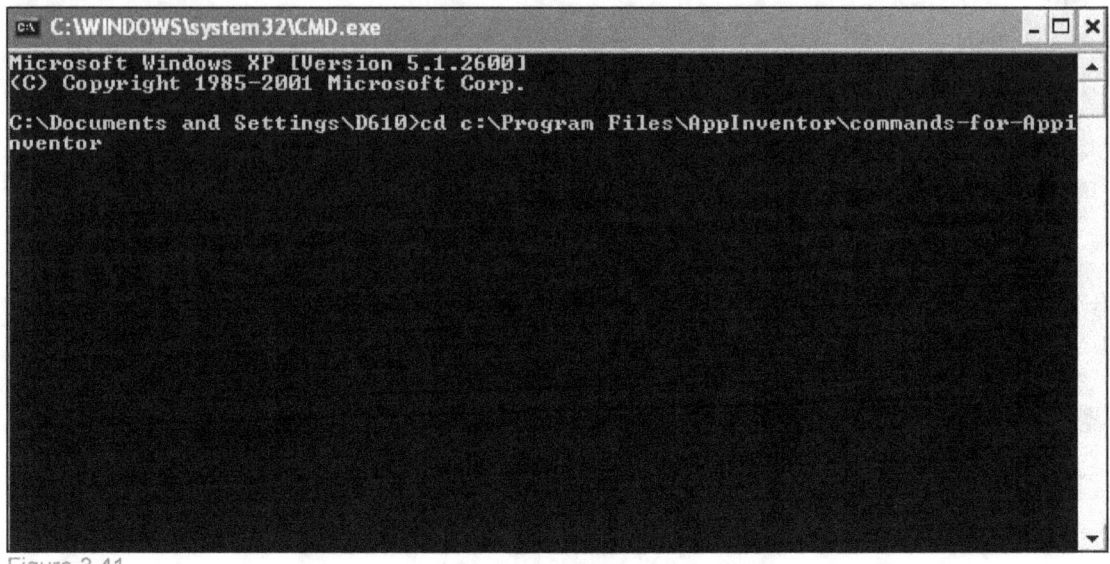

Figure 3.41

Next type "adb devices" and hit Enter. Notice there is information under "List of devices attached". Your device information may be different but if you see any information, then you have successfully installed your device driver and your PC is communicating with your phone. See Figure 3.42.

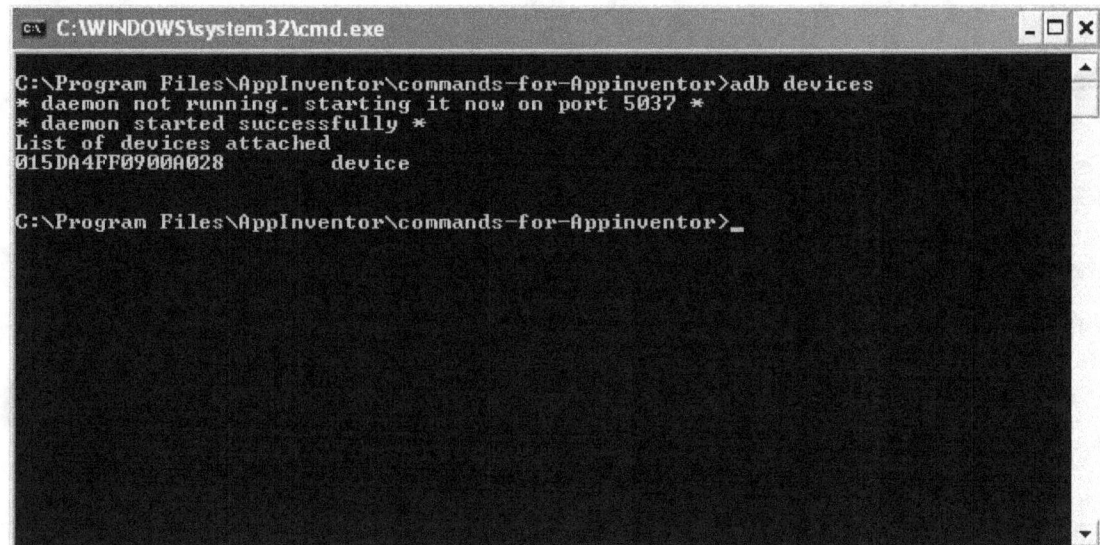

Figure 3.42

If you still are having issues with device driver installation visit Google Labs at:

http://appinventor.googlelabs.com/learn/setup/windows-drivers.html

Remember, App Inventor is a Beta product, thus, there will be many roadblocks.

Launching App Inventor

Next, let's launch App Inventor. You must have a Google account to use App Inventor. If you do not have a Google Account sign up for a free account by visiting Gmail.com.

App Inventor is launched from your web browser by visiting:

http://appinventor.googlelabs.com/

Next click "My Projects".

App Inventor will launch. Next, click New to create a new project. See Figure 3.43.

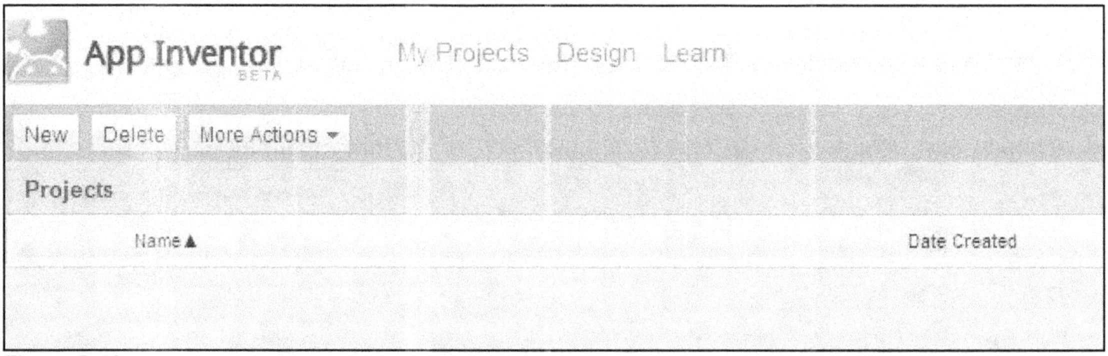

Figure 3.43

I name my project P1, then click OK. See Figure 3.44.

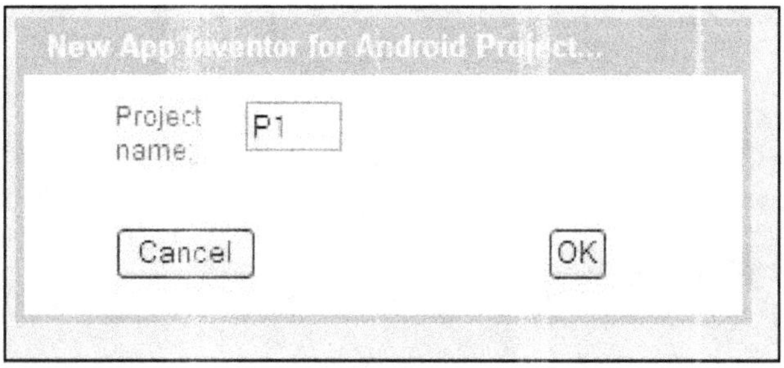

Figure 3.44

Next, you will be in the <u>App Inventor Designer</u> area also known as Designer for short. Later, I will explain the features of App Inventor Designer in detail. See Figure 3.45.

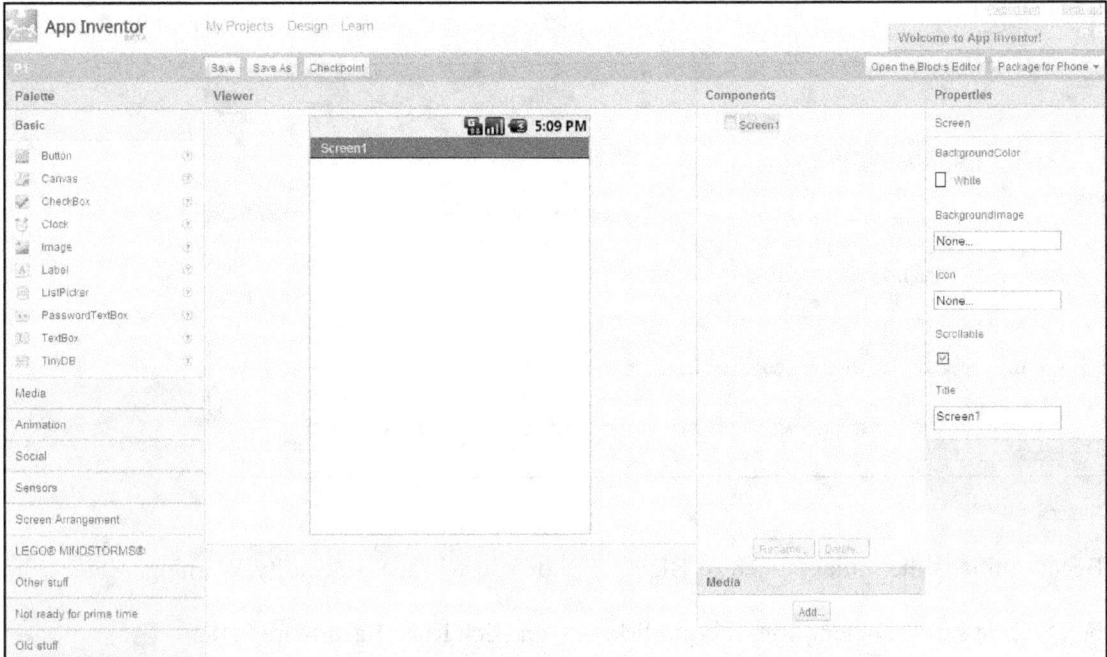

Figure 3.45

Next click "Open the Blocks Editor" in the upper right corner. See Figure 3.46.

Figure 3.46

On your initial launch of Blocks Editor, you will see the "Launching application" java message. See Figure 3.47.

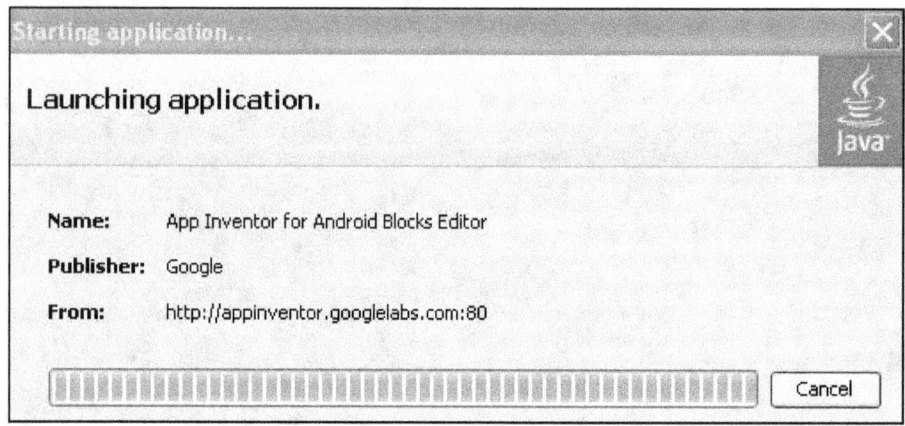

Figure 3.47

Because this is the initial launch of Blocks Editor you will get a Security Warning. Check the box "Always trust content from this publisher" then click Run. See Figure 3.48.

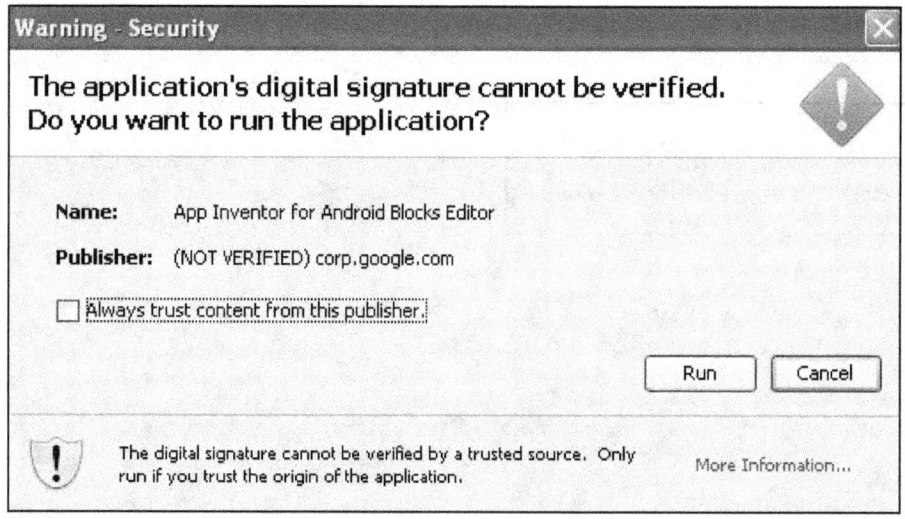

Figure 3.48

Next, we have the option to "Use a phone", "Use the emulator" or "Continue without a device". If you have a phone an Android phone that you have tested and connected then I recommend selecting "Use a phone". If you do not have an Android phone connected select "Use the emulator". App Inventor allows you to create applications without having a physical phone. I have a phone but I want to show you the emulator so I click "Use the emulator".

See Figure 3.49.

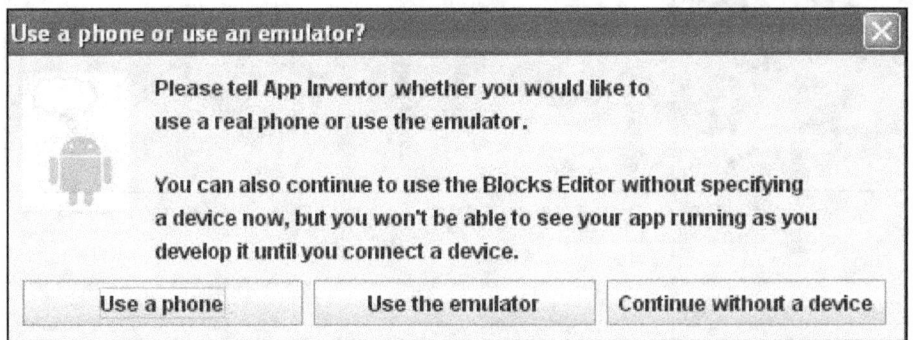

Figure 3.49

I have my phone connected so App Inventor gives me a choice. Next, I click "Start running an emulator. I'm unplugging my phone.". See Figure 3.50.

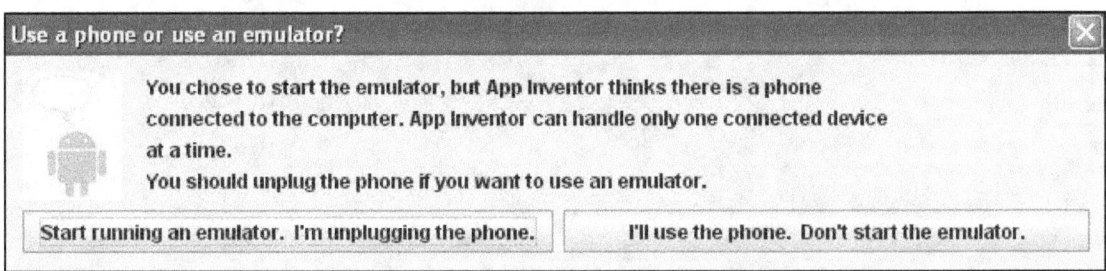

Figure 3.50

Next, we see "Starting the emulator. Please be patient". Click OK to continue. See Figure 3.51.

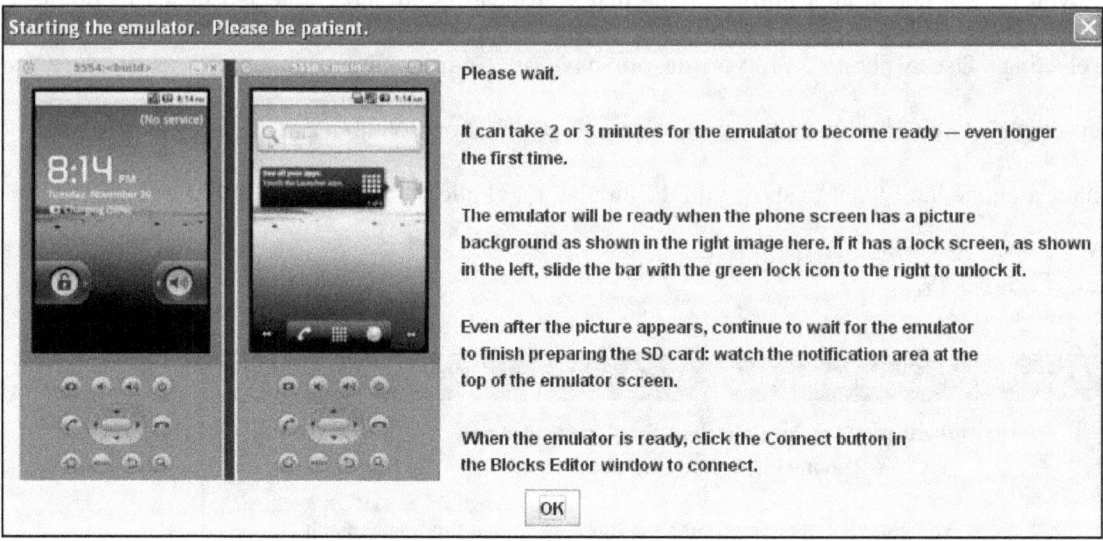

Figure 3.51

Next, App Inventor for Android Blocks Editor (Blocks Editor for short) launches. Later, I will

explain in detail the features of Blocks Editor. See Figure 3.52.

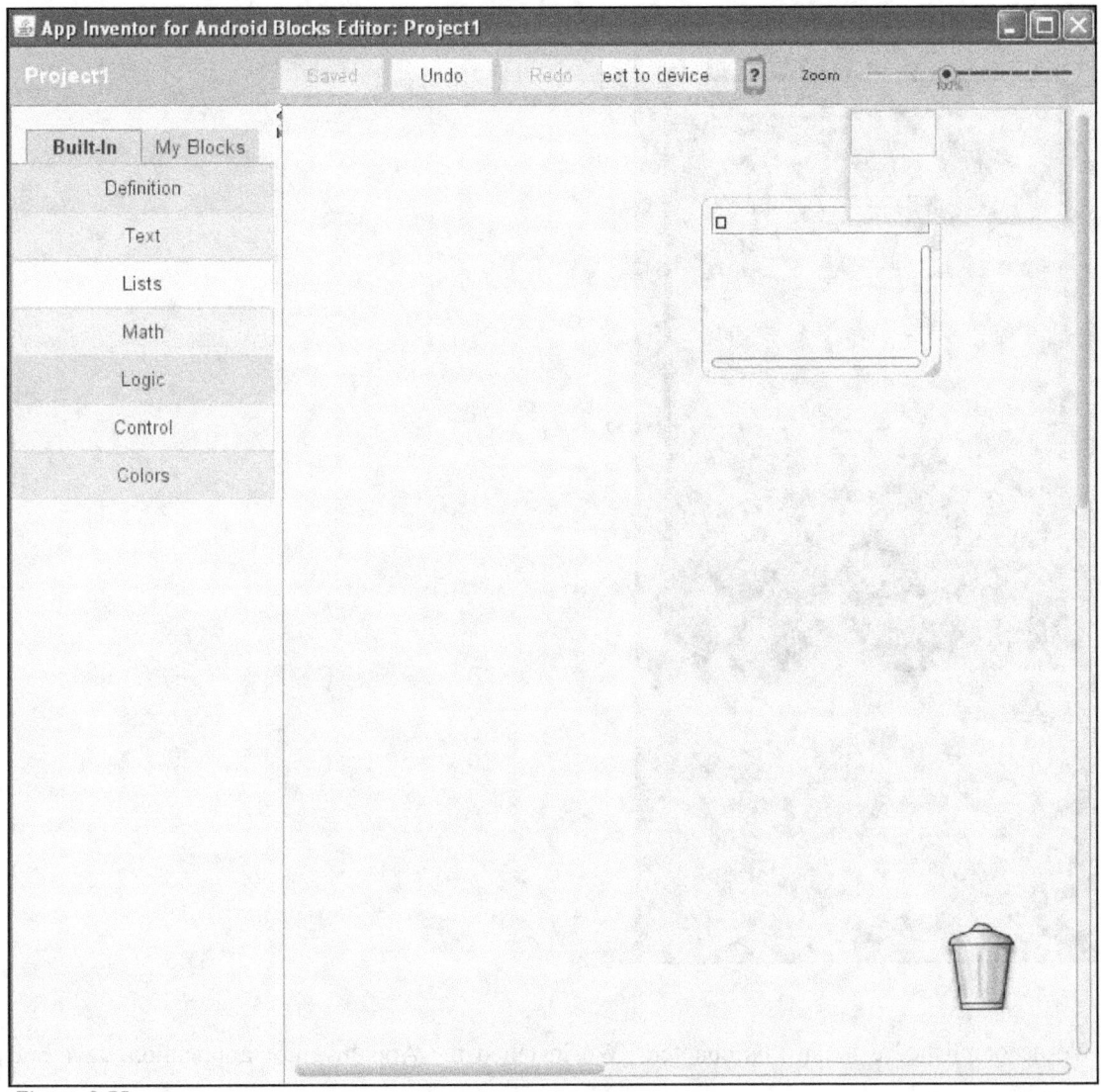

Figure 3.52

In Figure 3.53, Notice the emulator. The emulator behaves similarly to an actual phone. Once you develop an application, the emulator will run it accordingly.

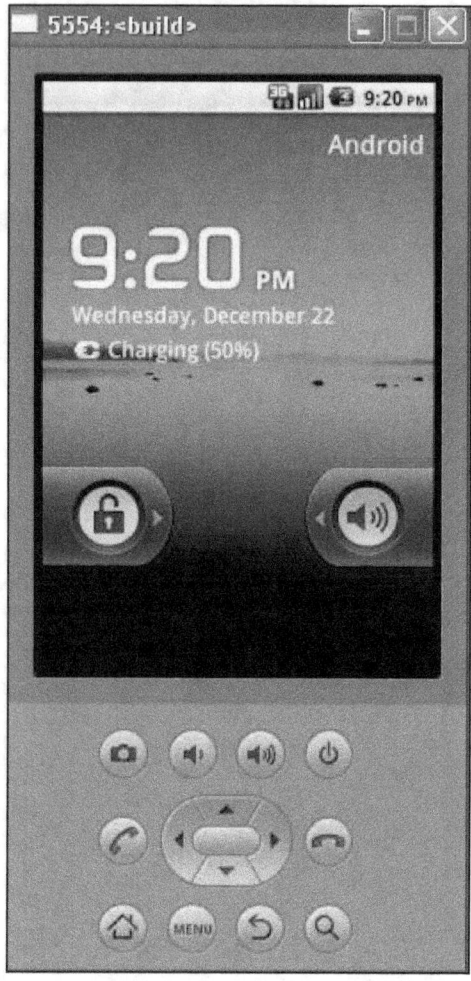

Figure 3.53

We accomplished a lot in this chapter. We installed the App Inventor application, Java and PDANet. In the next chapter, I will explain App Inventor Designer in detail.

4

Overview of The App Inventor Designer

The App Inventor Designer is where you create the layout and select the components for your application. The App Inventor Blocks Editor is where you assemble program blocks that specify how the components should behave. With the Blocks Editor, you assemble programs visually, putting the pieces together like a jigsaw puzzle. The App Inventor Designer is analogous to the ingredients in a cooking recipe while the App Inventor Blocks Editor is analogous to instructions in a cooking recipe.

Designer is divided into the following sections: Palette, Viewer, Components and Properties.

Palette

Palette is divided into 10 categories which are Basic, Media, Animation, Social, Sensors, Screen Arrangement, LEGO® MINDSTORMS® , Other Stuff, Not Ready for Prime Time and Old Stuff. Each category has features which I will explain below.

In Figure 4.1, notice Basic has the following components: Button, Canvas, CheckBox, Clock, Image, Label, ListPicker, PasswordTextBox, TextBox, and TinyDB.

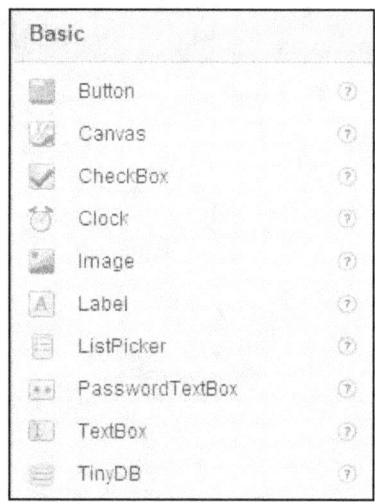

Figure 4.1

Button

The button gives your application the ability to detect clicks. Many aspects of the button's appearance can be changed. In addition, the ability to be clickable can be changed in Designer.

Canvas

The canvas is a two-dimensional touch-sensitive rectangular panel which allows drawing. In addition, sprites can be moved.

Clock

The clock is a non-visible component. It is the phone's clock. It is a timer and it provides time calculations.

Image

Image is a component for displaying images.

Label

A Label displays a piece of text, which is specified through the text property.

ListPicker

A button that once clicked, displays a list of text for the user to select.

PasswordTextBox

This is a box for entering passwords. This is the same as the TextBox component except PasswordTextBox does not display the characters typed by the user.

TextBox

Textbox a box for the user to enter text.

TinyDB

This is a non-visible component and database that stores values on the phone.

In Figure 4.2, notice the Media components: Camera, ImagePicker, Player, Sound and VideoPlayer.

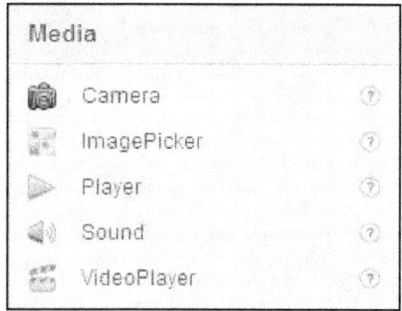

Figure 4.2

Camera

The camera component is used to take pictures using the device's camera. After the picture is taken, the name of the file on the phone containing the picture is available as an argument to the AfterPicture event.

ImagePicker

When the user clicks an image picker button, the device's image gallery appears, and the user can choose an image. After the user picks an image, the property ImagePath is set to a name that designates the image.

Player

The player is a multimedia component that plays audio or video and controls phone vibration.

Sound

Sound is a multimedia component that plays sound files and vibrates for a specified time that is set in the Blocks Editor.

VideoPlayer

VideoPlayer is a multimedia component capable of playing videos.

In Figure 4.3, notice the Animation components: Ball and ImageSprite which both use the term Sprite. A Sprite [9] is a two dimensional graphic or animation.

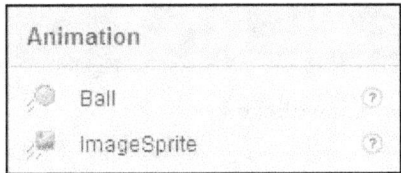

Figure 4.3

Ball

A ball is a round sprite that can be placed on a canvas.

ImageSprite

An ImageSprite is a sprite that can be placed on a Canvas, where it can react to touches, drags and interact with other sprites.

In Figure 4.4, notice the Social components: ContactPicker, EmailPicker, PhoneCall, PhoneNumberPicker, Texting and Twitter.

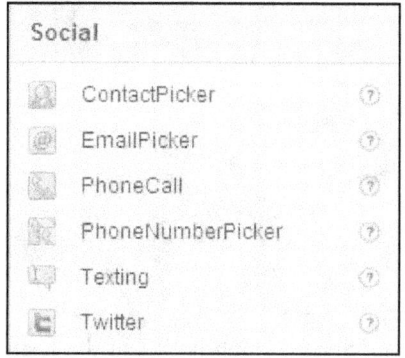

Figure 4.4

ContactPicker

ContactPicker is a button that displays a list of the contacts after being clicked.

EmailPicker

EmailPicker is a text box used for adding the email address of a contact. The component contains the auto-completion feature.

PhoneCall

PhoneCall is a non-visible component that makes a phone call to the number specified in the PhoneNumber property.

PhoneNumberPicker

PhoneNumberPicker is a button that displays a list of the contacts' phone numbers after being clicked.

Texting

Texting is a component that will send the text message specified in the message property to the phone number specified in the PhoneNumber property.

Twitter

Twitter is a non-visible component that facilitates communication with Twitter.

In Figure 4.5, notice the Sensors components: AccelerometerSensor, LocationSensor and OrientationSensor.

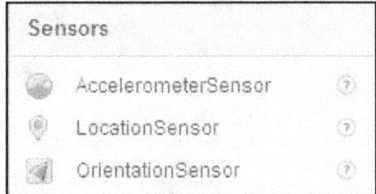

Figure 4.5

AccelerometerSensor

The AccelerometerSensor is a non-visible component that can detect shaking and measure acceleration.

LocationSensor

The LocationSensor is non-visible component providing location information. This includes longitude, latitude, altitude (if supported by the device), and address.

OrientationSensor

The OrientationSensor is a non-visible component which provides physical orientation information about the devices in three dimensions,

In Figure 4.6, notice the Screen Arrangement components: HorizontalArrangement, TableArrangement and VerticalArrangement.

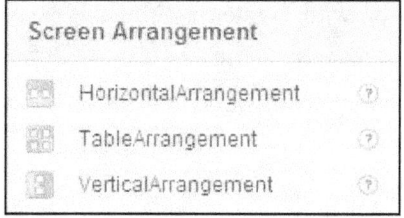

Figure 4.6

HorizontalArrangement

HorizontalArrangement allows the developer to format components from left to right.

TableArrangement

TableArrangement is a formatting element in which allows components to be displayed in tabular form.

VerticalArrangement

VerticalArrangement allows the developer to format components up and down.

In this book, we are not going to cover LEGO® MINDSTORMS® (Figure 4.7).

Figure 4.7

These components provide control of LEGO® MINDSTORMS® NXT robots using Bluetooth.

LEGO® MINDSTORMS® are programmable robotic toys manufactured by the Lego Group 10.

Below is an image of a LEGO® MINDSTORMS® robot. See Figure 4.8

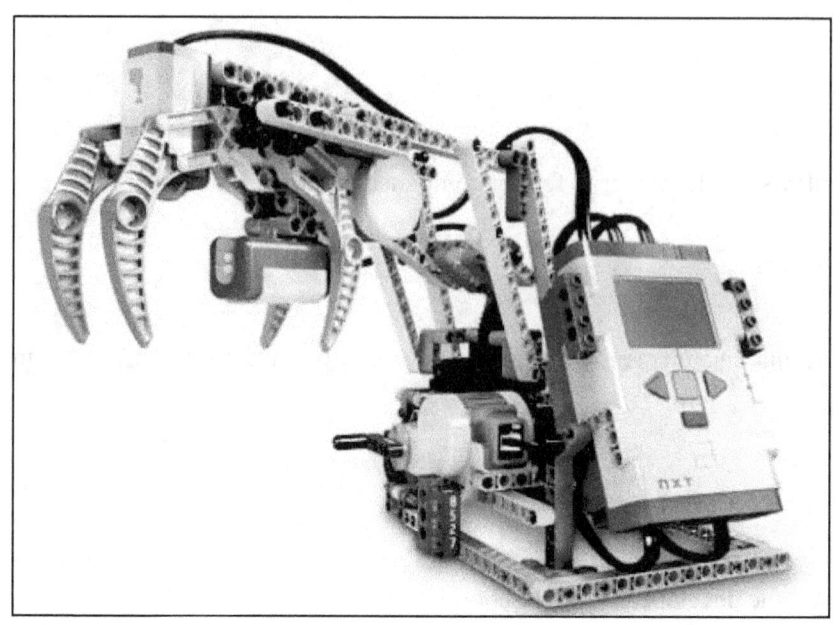

Figure 4.8

In Figure 4.9, notice other stuff: ActivityStarter, BarcodeScanner, Notifier, SpeechRecognizer and TextToSpeech.

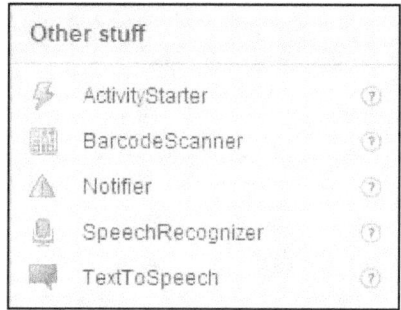

Figure 4.9

ActivityStarter

ActivityStarter is a component that can launch an activity such as:

- starting another App Inventor for Android application

- starting the camera application

- performing web search

- opening the web browser to a specified URL

- opening the map application to a specified location

BarcodeScanner

BarcodeScanner is a component for reading barcodes.

Notifier

The Notifier is a component that creates alert messages.

SpeechRecognizer

SpeechRecognizer is a component for using voice recognition to convert from speech to text.

TextToSpeech

TextToSpeech is a component that allows the device to speak text audibly.

In Figure 4.10, notice "Not ready for prime time": BluetoothClient, BluetoothServer, GameClient, SoundRecorder, TinyWebDB and Voting. "Not ready for prime time" consists of components which are still being tested.

Figure 4.10

BluetoothClient

Bluetooth client component

BluetoothServer

Bluetooth server component

GameClient

GameClient provides a way for applications to communicate with online game servers.

SoundRecorder

SoundRecorder is multimedia component that records audio.

TinyWebDB

TinyWebDB is non-visible component that communicates with a Web service to store and retrieve information.

Voting

The Voting component allows users to vote on a question by communicating with a Web service.

Viewer

Viewer is where we assemble images, buttons and other visible components. The non-visible components are represented below the viewer. See Figure 4.11.

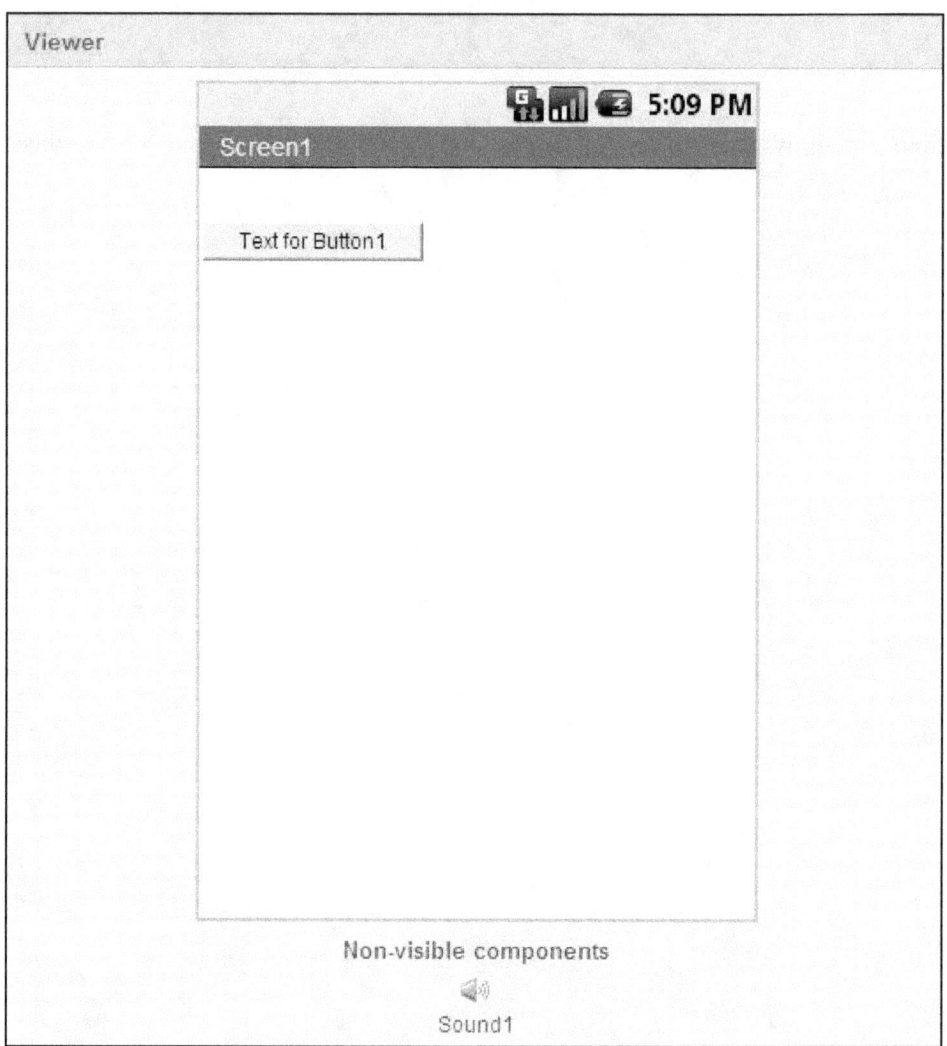

Figure 4.11

Components

The Components section allows us to gather components such as labels, buttons and sounds. See

Figure 4.12.

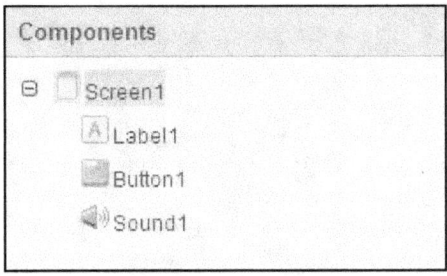

Figure 4.12

The Media section allows us to add media. See Figure 4.13.

Figure 4.13

Properties

The Properties section allows us to change screen attributes such as background color and background images. See Figure 4.14.

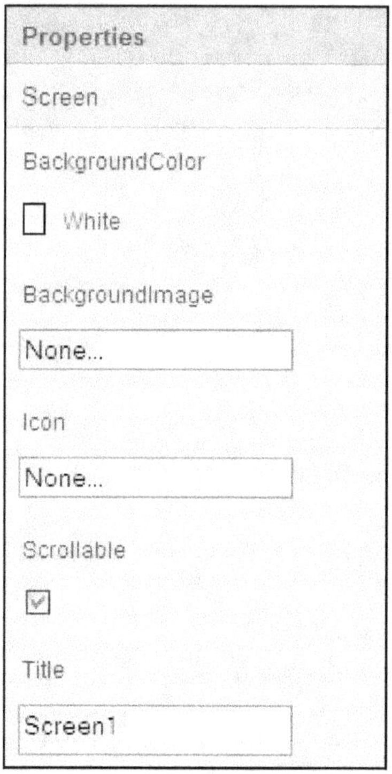

Properties
Screen
BackgroundColor
☐ White
BackgroundImage
None...
Icon
None...
Scrollable
☑
Title
Screen1

Figure 4.14

In this chapter we did an overview of App Inventor Designer which directly compliments Blocks and Components. Next we will do an overview of the Blocks Editor.

5

Overview of

Blocks Editor

Built-in Blocks

As we stated in the previous chapter, the App Inventor Blocks Editor is where you assemble program blocks that specify how the components should behave. With the Blocks Editor, you assemble programs visually, putting the pieces together like a jigsaw puzzle. The App Inventor Blocks Editor is analogous to instructions in a cooking recipe.

The Blocks Editor has 7 sections for built-in blocks which are:

- Definition Blocks

- Text Blocks

- List Blocks

- Math Blocks

- Logic Blocks

- Control Blocks

- Color Blocks

Definition Blocks

Definition Blocks are mainly used for grouping other blocks. Definition Blocks contain the following blocks:

- procedure
- procedureWithResult
- name
- variable

procedure

This block allows the developer to group many blocks together. The developer can call the procedure block to execute the other blocks with in procedure. See Figure 5.1.

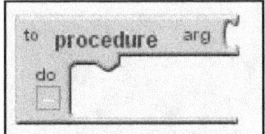

Figure 5.1

procedureWithResult

This block is the same as procedure except a result is returned upon execution. See Figure 5.2.

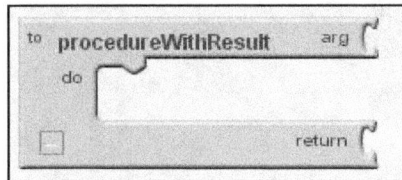

Figure 5.2

name

This block allows you to name your procedure. By default, App Inventor assigns unique names to procedures. See Figure 5.3.

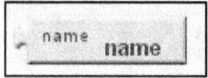

Figure 5.3

variable

This block stores values that can be changed during the execution of your application. See Figure 5.4.

Figure 5.4

Text Blocks

Text Blocks are blocks that contain text and these blocks manipulate text. Text Blocks contain the following blocks:

- text
- =
- join
- make text
- length
- text<
- text=
- text>
- upcase
- downcase
- trim
- starts at
- contains
- splitatfirst
- split at first of any
- split
- split at any
- split at spaces

- segment

text

The text block simply contains a text string. See Figure 5.5.

Figure 5.5

=

The equals block checks whether 2 values are equal. If the values are equal, then the block returns a value of "true". If the values are not equal, then the block returns a value of "false". See Figure 5.6.

Figure 5.6

join

The join block appends the contents of the 2nd block to the 1st block. See Figure 5.7.

Figure 5.7

make text

The make text block joins all values into one text string. See Figure 5.8.

Figure 5.8

length

The length block returns the length of text string. See Figure 5.9.

Figure 5.9

text<

The text< block tells whether the 1st text string is alphabetically less than the 2nd text string. See Figure 5.10.

Figure 5.10

text=

The text= block tells whether the text strings are the same. See Figure 5.11.

Figure 5.11

text>

The text> block tells whether the 1st text string is alphabetically greater than the 2nd text string. See Figure 5.12.

Figure 5.12

upcase

The upcase block returns a copy of the text string in all upper case. See Figure 5.13.

Figure 5.13

downcase

The downcase block returns a copy of the text string in all lower case. See Figure 5.14.

Figure 5.14

trim

The trim block returns a copy of the text string removing any leading or trailing spaces. See Figure 5.15.

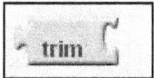

Figure 5.15

starts at

The start at block returns the character position of a given string of text. (Example: "ed" appears in position 3 for Sled and Fred. Thus 3 would be returned). See Figure 5.16.

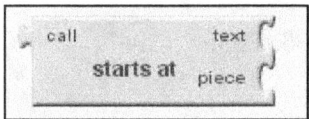

Figure 5.16

contains

The contains block will return a value of true if the text string appears in the text string "piece". See Figure 5.17.

Figure 5.17

splitatfirst

The splitatfirstblock block divides text into 2 items at the specified location. See Figure 5.18.

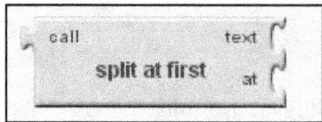

Figure 5.18

split at first of any

The "split at first of any" block divides text string into 2 lists with the location of any item in the list as a dividing point. See Figure 5.19.

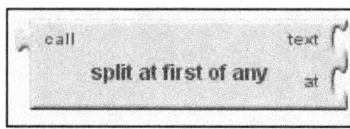

Figure 5.19

split

The split block divides text into pieces using "at" as the diving point. See Figure 5.20.

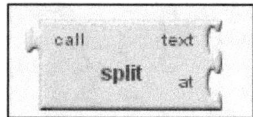

Figure 5.20

split at any

The "split at any" block divides text into a list using any of the items in "at" as the diving point. See Figure 5.21.

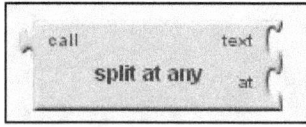

Figure 5.21

split at spaces

The "split at spaces" block divides text at the spaces. See Figure 5.22.

Figure 5.22

segment

The segment block extracts part of the text starting at the "start" position. See Figure 5.23.

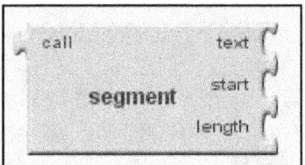

Figure 5.23

List Blocks

List Blocks are blocks that allow the developer to create and manipulate lists. List Blocks contain the following blocks:

- make a list
- select list item
- replace list item
- remove list item
- length of list
- append to list
- add items to list
- is in list?
- position in list
- pick random item
- is list empty?
- is a list?

make a list

The "make a list" block creates a list from the block inputs. See Figure 5.24.

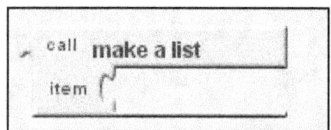

Figure 5.24

select list item

The "select list item" block selects the list item at the designated location. See Figure 5.25.

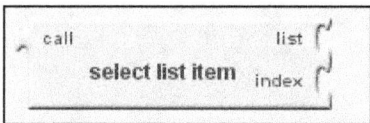

Figure 5.25

replace list item

The "replace list item" block inserts "replacement" into the designated location. See Figure 5.26.

Figure 5.26

remove list item

The "remove list item" block removes the item from the list. See Figure 5.27.

Figure 5.27

length of list

The "length of list" block gives the number of items in the list. See Figure 5.28.

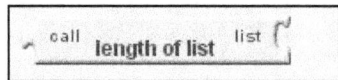

Figure 5.28

append to list

The "append to list" block appends to the end of the list. See Figure 5.29.

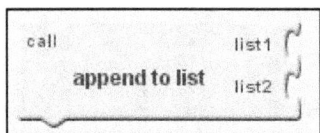

Figure 5.29

add items to list

The "add items to list" block adds items to the list. See Figure 5.30.

Figure 5.30

is in list?

The "is in list?" block determines whether a specific item is in the list. See Figure 5.31.

Figure 5.31

position in list

The "position in list" block determines the position of an item in the list. See Figure 5.32.

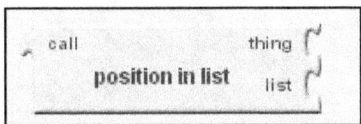

Figure 5.32

pick random item

The "pick random item" block selects a random item within the list. See Figure 5.33.

Figure 5.33

is list empty?

The "is list empty?" block determines whether or not the list is empty. See Figure 5.34.

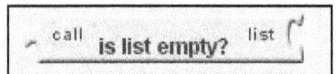

Figure 5.34

is a list?

The "is a list?" block determines whether the item is a list. See Figure 5.35

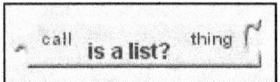

Figure 5.35

82

Math Blocks

Math Blocks are used to perform mathematical functions. Math Blocks contain the following blocks:

- number
- >
- <
- <=
- >=
- equals
- +
- -
- x
- /
- sqrt
- random fraction
- random integer
- random set seed
- negate
- min
- max
- quotient

- remainder

- modulo

- abs

- round

- floor

- ceiling

- exp

- log

- sin

- cos

- tan

- asin

- acos

- atan

- atan2

- format as decimal

- is a number?

number

The number block specifies a numeric value. See Figure 5.36.

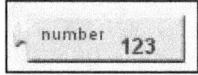

Figure 5.36

>

The ">" block compares 2 numbers. If the 1st number is greater than the 2nd number then it returns true. If not, then it returns false. See Figure 5.37.

Figure 5.37

<

The "<" block compares 2 numbers. If the 1st number is less than the 2nd number then it returns true. If not, then it returns false. See Figure 5.38.

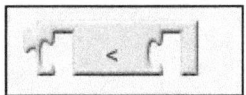

Figure 5.38

<=

The "<=" block compares 2 numbers. If the 1st number is less than or equal to the 2nd number then it returns true. If not, then it returns false. See Figure 5.39.

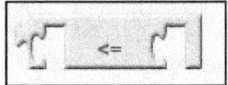

Figure 5.39

>=

The ">=" block compares 2 numbers. If the 1st number is greater than or equal to the 2nd number then it returns true. If not, then it returns false. See Figure 5.40.

Figure 5.40

equals

The equals block compares 2 numbers. If the 1st number is equal to the 2nd number then it returns true. If not, then it returns false See Figure 5.41.

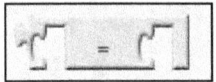

Figure 5.41

+

The "+" block returns the sum of adding 2 numbers.   See Figure 5.42.

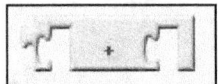

Figure 5.42

-

The "-" block returns the results of subtracting the 2nd number from the 1st number. See Figure 5.43.

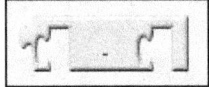

Figure 5.43

x

The "x" block returns the results of multiplying 2 numbers. See Figure 5.44.

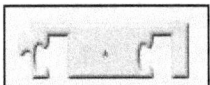

Figure 5.44

/

The "/" block returns the results of dividing 2 numbers. See Figure 5.45.

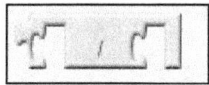

Figure 5.45

sqrt

The sqrt block gives the square root of the number. See Figure 5.46.

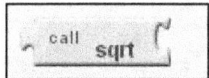

Figure 5.46

random fraction

The "random fraction" block returns a random value between 0 and 1. See Figure 5.47.

Figure 5.47

random integer

The "random integer" block returns a random integer between the input values. See Figure 5.48.

Figure 5.48

random set seed

The "random set seed" block is used to create repeatable sequences of random numbers. See Figure 5.49.

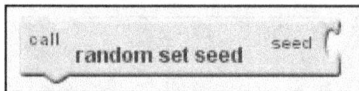

Figure 5.49

negate

The negate block returns the negative of the input number. See Figure 5.50.

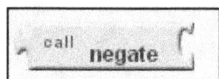

Figure 5.50

min

The min block returns the smallest of a given set of numbers. See Figure 5.51.

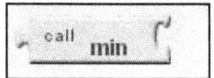

Figure 5.51

max

The max block returns the largest of a given set of numbers.   See Figure 5.52.

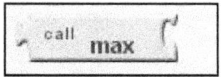

Figure 5.52

quotient

The quotient block returns the result of dividing the 1st number by the 2nd number and truncating any decimals. See Figure 5.53.

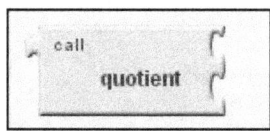

Figure 5.53

remainder

The remainder block returns the remainder of dividing the 1st number by the 2nd number. See Figure 5.54.

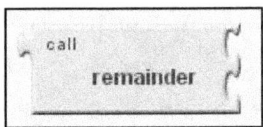

Figure 5.54

abs

The abs block returns the absolute value of the input. See Figure 5.55.

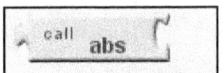

Figure 5.55

round

The round block rounds the input to the nearest integer and returns the result. See Figure 5.56.

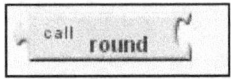

Figure 5.56

floor

The floor block returns the greatest integer that is less than or equal to the input. See Figure 5.57.

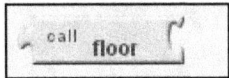

Figure 5.57

ceiling

The ceiling block returns the smallest integer that is greater than or equal to the input. See Figure 5.58.

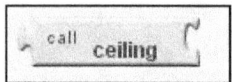

Figure 5.58

exp

The exp block returns e (2.71828...) raised to the power of the input. See Figure 5.59.

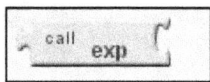

Figure 5.59

log

The log block returns the natural logarithm of the input. See Figure 5.60.

Figure 5.60

sin

The sin block returns the sine of the input. See Figure 5.61.

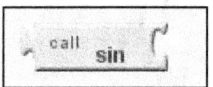

Figure 5.61

cos

The cos block returns the cosine of the input. See Figure 5.62.

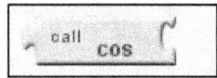

Figure 5.62

tan

The tan block returns the tangent of the input. See Figure 5.63.

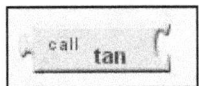

Figure 5.63

asin

The asin block returns the arcsine of the input. See Figure 5.64.

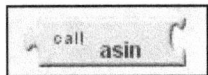

Figure 5.64

acos

The acos block returns the arccosine of the input.   See Figure 5.65.

Figure 5.65

atan

The atan block returns the arctangent of the input. See Figure 5.66.

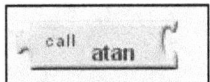

Figure 5.66

atan2

The atan2 block returns the arctangent of the inputs. See Figure 5.67.

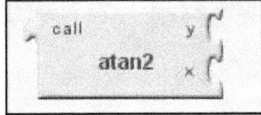

Figure 5.67

format as decimal

The "format as decimal" block formats the input as a decimal with a specific amount of places after the decimal point. See Figure 5.68.

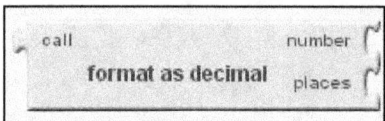

Figure 5.68

is a number?

The "is a number?" block returns true if the input is a number. See Figure 5.70.

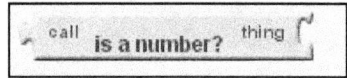

Figure 5.70

Logic Blocks

Logic Blocks are used to perform logical functions. Logic Blocks contain the following blocks:

- true

- false

- not

- =

- and

- or

true

The true block represents the constant value of true. Use this block to set a variable as true. See Figure 5.71.

Figure 5.71

false

The false block represents the constant value of false. Use this block to set a variable as false. See Figure 5.72.

Figure 5.72

not

The not block negates a value. It turns true to false and false to true. See Figure 5.73.

Figure 5.73

=

The = block checks to see whether its inputs are equal.   See Figure 5.74.

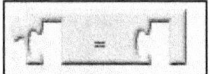

Figure 5.74

and

The and block checks whether all input conditions are true. The result is true if and only if all

the inputs are true.   See Figure 5.75.

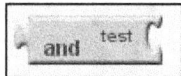

Figure 5.75

<u>or</u>

The or block checks whether all input conditions are true. The result is true if one or more of the inputs are true. See Figure 5.76.

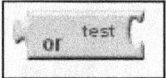

Figure 5.76

Control Blocks

Control Blocks act as conditional statements which determine outcomes.   Control Blocks contain the following blocks:

- if
- ifelse
- choose
- foreach
- while
- get start text
- close screen
- close screen with result

if

The if block checks if an input is true. If the input is true then it performs the designated actions. See Figure 5.77.

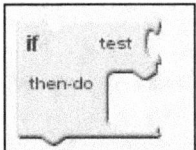

Figure 5.77

ifelse

The ifelse block checks if an input is true. If the input is true, then it performs the designated actions. If the input is false, then the else action is performed. See Figure 5.78.

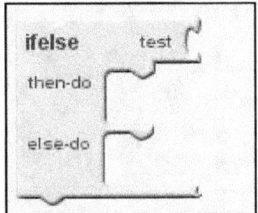

Figure 5.78

choose

The choose block checks if an input is true. If the input is true then it performs the designated actions and returns a value. See Figure 5.79.

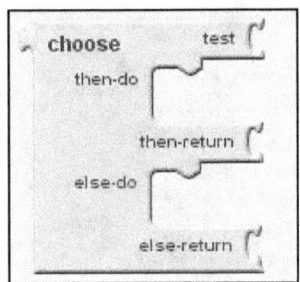

Figure 5.79

foreach

The foreach block performs the action stated in "do" for each item in the list. See Figure 5.80.

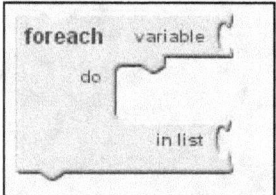

Figure 5.80

while

The while block checks the condition. If true, this block performs the action given in "do" and the process starts over. If false, the block ends. See Figure 5.81.

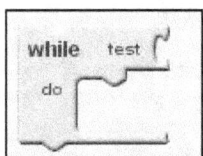

Figure 5.81

get start text

The get start text block returns the text passed to the application when the application was started. See Figure 5.82.

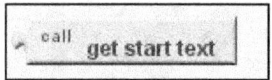

Figure 5.82

close screen

The close screen block closes the application. See Figure 5.83.

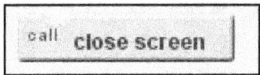

Figure 5.83

close screen with result

The close screen with result block closes the application and sets the variable APP_INVENTOR_RESULT to the given value. See Figure 5.84.

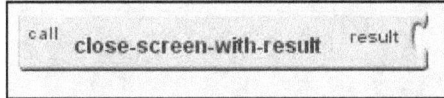

Figure 5.84

Color Blocks

The Color Blocks section contains blocks for common colors.

These include:

- None

- Black

- Blue

- Cyan

- Dark Gray

- Gray

- Green

- Light Gray

- Magenta

- Orange

- Pink

- Red

- White

- Yellow

See Figure 5.85

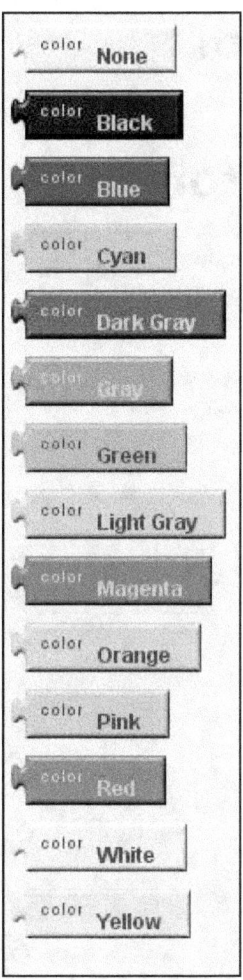

Figure 5.85

You can use Color Blocks for parts of your application that require color.

There are many blocks that can be used to create your application. This may seem overwhelming. The good news is that you probably won't use most of these blocks. How often does on need to calculate the tangent of an angle for an application? It probably doesn't happen very often. If you desire to create your own application, then you should focus on your application and try to understand the blocks that pertain to its functions.

6

Overview of

Blocks Editor

My Blocks

In the last chapter we covered Built-in Blocks. In this chapter, we will be covering "My Blocks". The Blocks Editor has 2 main sections for blocks. One is called "Built-in Blocks" (see previous chapter for details) and the other is "My Blocks". The main differences between "Built-in Blocks" and "My Blocks" are:

1) Built-in blocks are based on actual programming logic and commands.

2) My Blocks are based on selections that you determine in Designer. Thus, the Button Blocks will only be available in the Blocks Editor if you are using buttons in Designer.

Next, we will describe the different blocks available in "My Blocks".

Button

Button.Click

Button.Click indicates that a user has clicked on the button.   See Figure 6.1.

Button.GotFocus

Button.GotFocus indicates that the cursor has hovered over the button, thus making the button

clickable. See Figure 6.1.

Button.LostFocus

Button.LostFocus indicates that the cursor has hovered away from the button, thus making the

button un-clickable. See Figure 6.1.

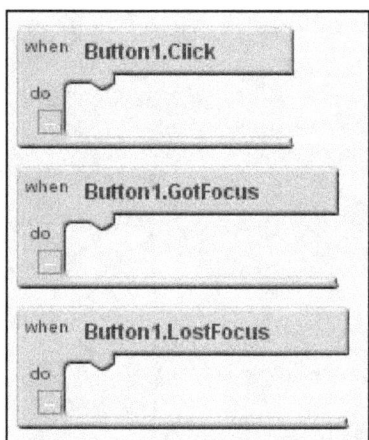

Figure 6.1

The following blocks report the value of the components property and Set the value of the

components property.

- Button.BackgroundColor

- Button.Enabled

- Button.Height

- Button.Image

- Button.Text

- Button.TextColor

- Button.Visible

See Figure 6.2.

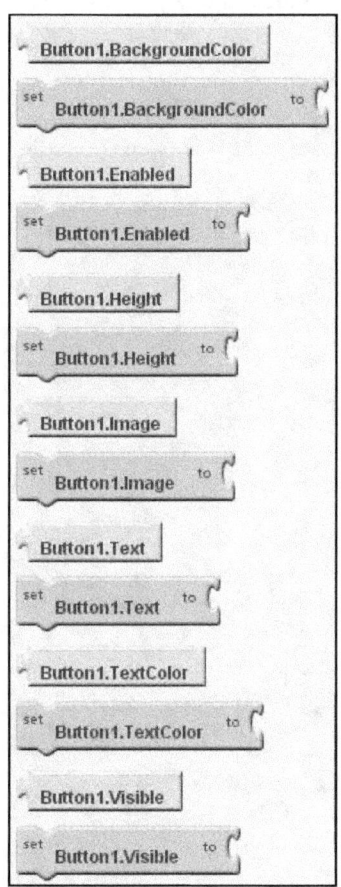

Figure 6.2

Canvas

Canvas.Dragged

When the user does a drag from one point (prevX, prevY) to another (x,y). The pair (startX, startY) indicates where the user first touched and "draggedSprite" indicates whether a sprite is being dragged. See Figure 6.3.

Canvas.Touched

When the user touches a canvas providing the (x,y) position of the touch relative to the upper left corner of the canvas. The value "touchSprite" is true if a sprite was also in this position. See Figure 6.3.

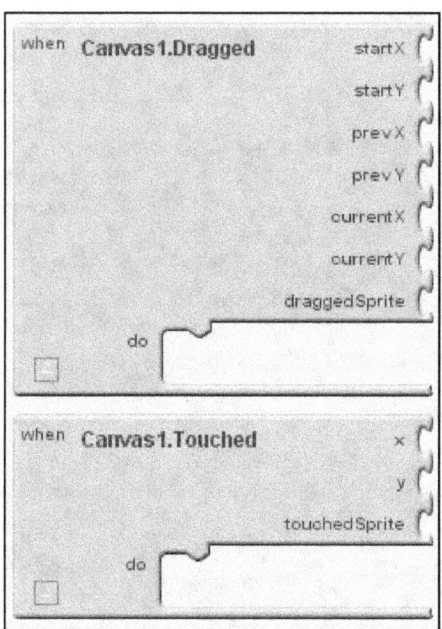

Figure 6.3

106

Canvas.Clear

Canvas.Clear clears the canvas without removing the background image.

Canvas.DrawCircle

Canvas.DrawCircle draws a circle on the canvas at the specified coordinates and radius.

Canvas.DrawLine

Canvas.DrawLine draws a line on the canvas between the specified coordinates.

Canvas.DrawPoint

Canvas.DrawPoint draws a point on the canvas at the specified coordinate.

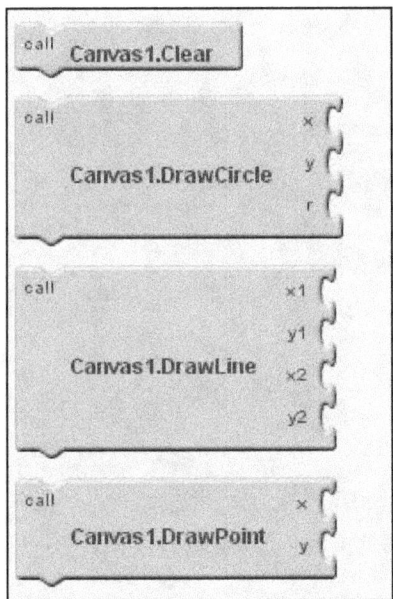

Figure 6.4

The following sets and reports the value of the component property.

Canvas.BackgroundColor

Canvas.BackgroundImage

Canvas.Height

Canvas.PaintColor

Canvas.Width

See Figure 6.5.

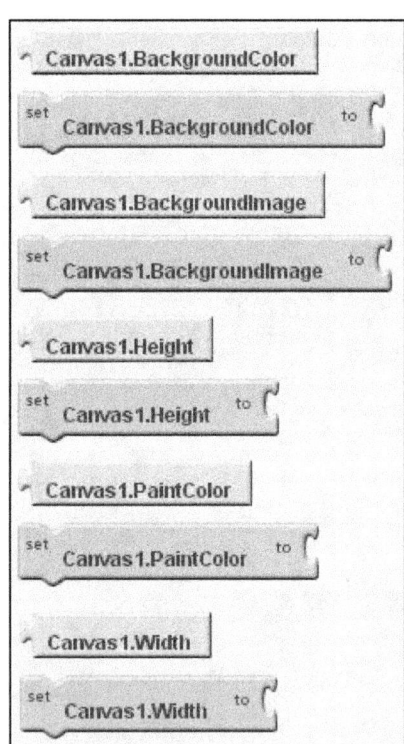

Figure 6.5

108

CheckBox

CheckBox.Changed, **CheckBox.GotFocus** and **CheckBox.LostFocus** are the default changed

event handlers. See Figure 6.6

Figure 6.6

The following sets and reports the value of the component property. See Figure 6.7.

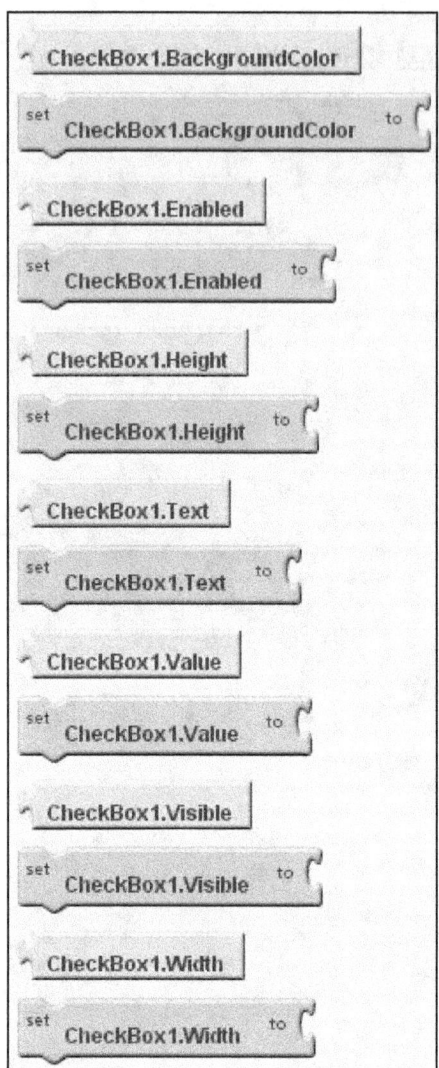

Figure 6.7

110

Clock

Clock.Timer activates the given block when the time has run out. See Figure 6.8.

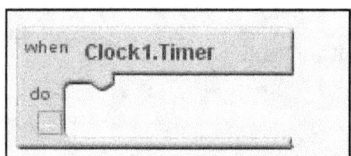

Figure 6.8

The following are instants in time after the given input. See Figure 6.9.

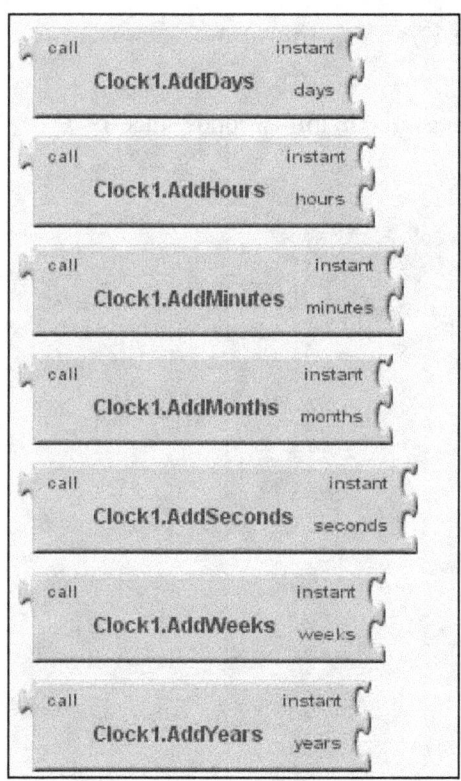

Figure 6.9

Clock.DayOfMonth is the actual day of the month.

Clock.Duration is the time between instants in milliseconds.

Clock.FormatDate is the text describing the date of an instant.

Clock.FormatDateTime is the text describing the date and time of an instant.

Clock.FormatTime is text describing the time of an instant.

ClockGetMillis is the instance of time as measured in milliseconds since 1970.

Clock.Hour is the hour of the day.

Clock.MakeInstant is the instant specified by MM/DD/YYYY.

Clock.MakeInstantFromMillis is the instance of time as measured in milliseconds since 1970.

See Figure 6.10.

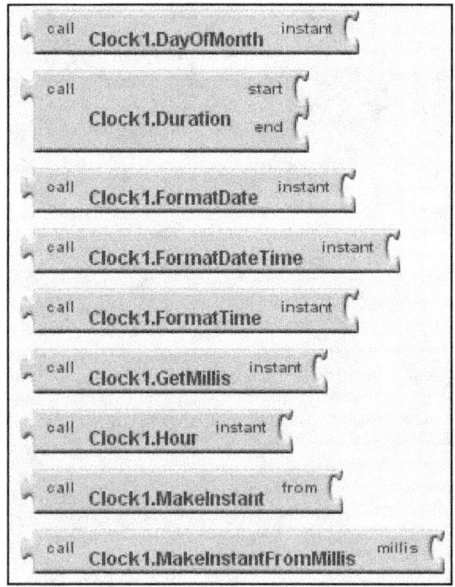

Figure 6.10

112

Clock.Minute is the minute of the hour.

Clock.Month is the month of the year.

ClockMonthName is the month name.

Clock.Now is the instant in time read from the phone's clock.

Clock.Second is the second of the minute.

Clock.SystemTime is the phone's internal time.

Clock.Weekday is the day of the week as represented by a number.

Clock.WeekdayName is the day of the week as represented by the name of the week day.

Clock.Year is the actual year.

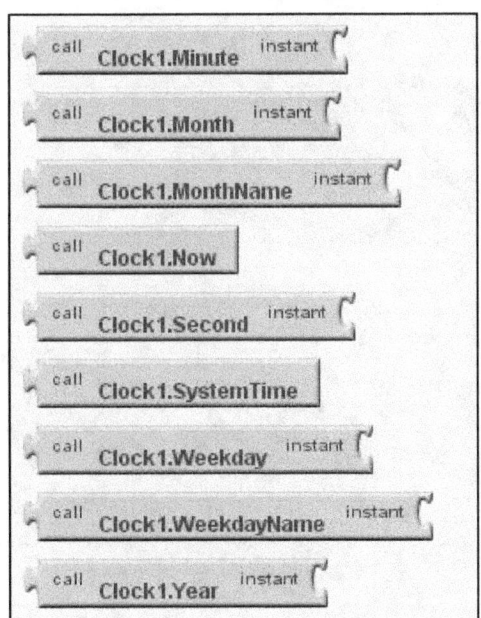

Figure 6.11

113

The following sets and reports the value of the components property: Clock.TimeAlwaysFires, Clock.TimerEnabled and ClockTimerInternal. See Figure 6.12.

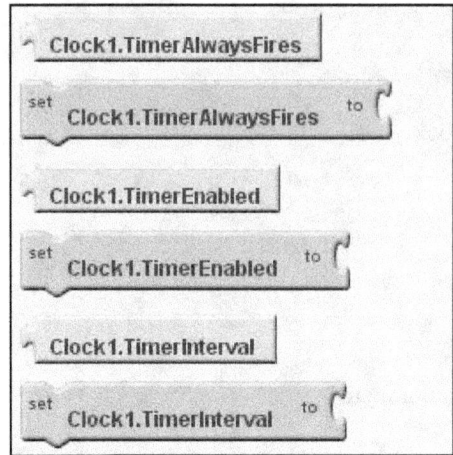

Figure 6.12

Image

The following sets and reports the value of the components property. See Figure 6.13.

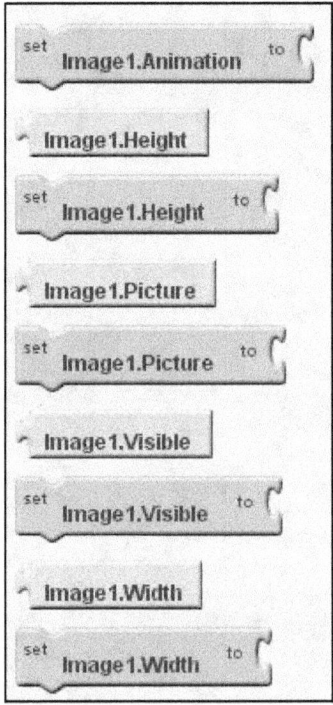

Figure 6.13

Label

The following sets and reports the value of the components property. See Figure 6.14.

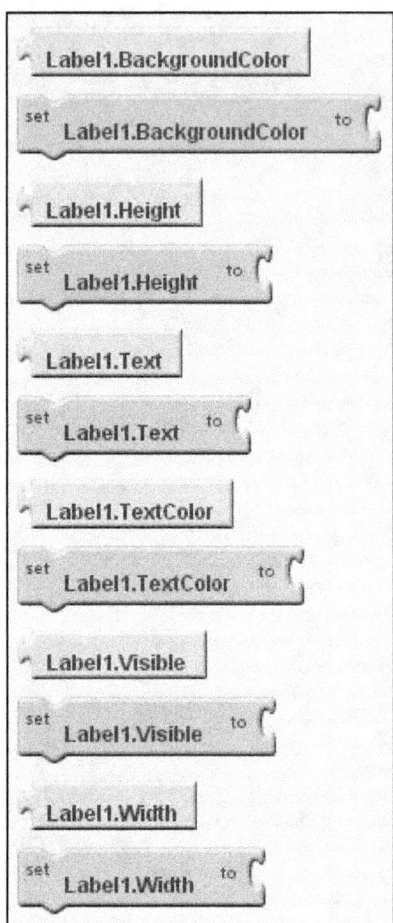

Figure 6.14

ListPicker

ListPicker.AfterPicking activates an event after the list picker returns its result and the properties have been filled in.

ListPicker.BeforePicking activates an event before the list picker returns its result and the properties have been filled in.

ListPicker.GotFocus indicates that the cursor has hovered over the button.

ListPicker.LostFocus indicates that the cursor has hovered away from the button.

See Figure 6.15.

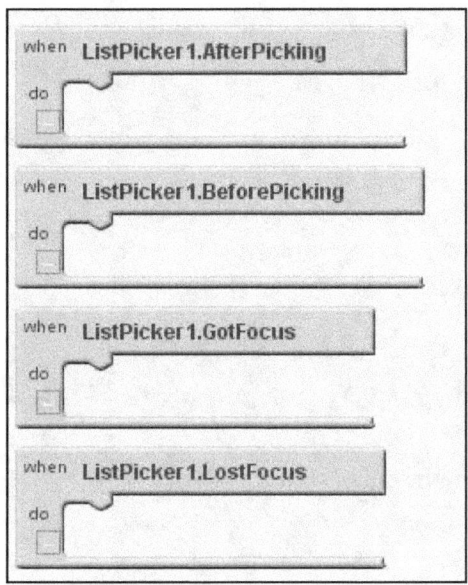

Figure 6.15

The following sets and reports the value of the components property. See Figure 6.16.

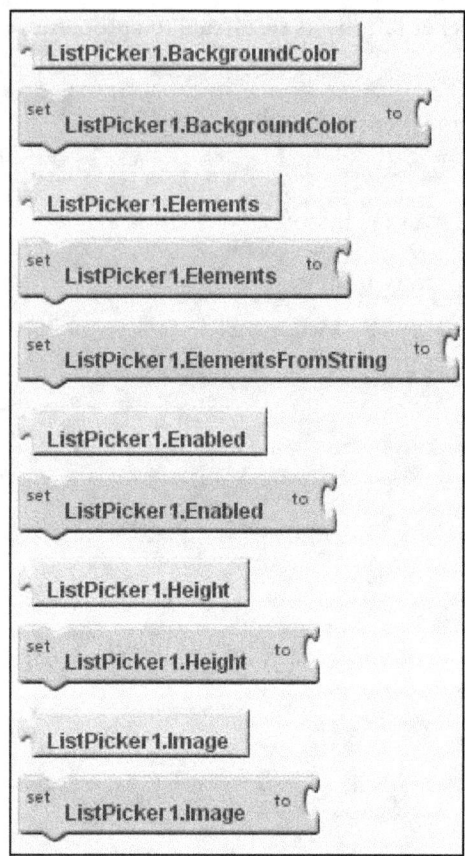

Figure 6.16

The following sets and reports the value of the components property. See Figure 6.17.

Figure 6.17

PasswordTextBox

PasswordTextBox.GotFocus is the default got focus event handler.

PasswordTextBox.LostFocus is the default lost focus event handler.

See Figure 6.18

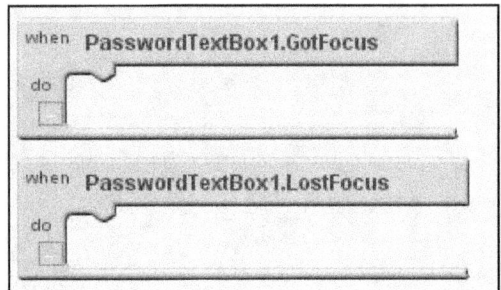

Figure 6.18

The following sets and reports the value of the components property. See Figure 6.19.

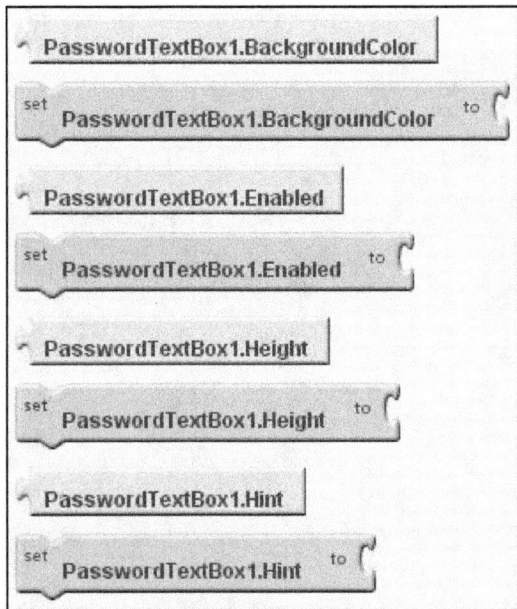

Figure 6.19

The following sets and reports the value of the components property. See Figure 6.20.

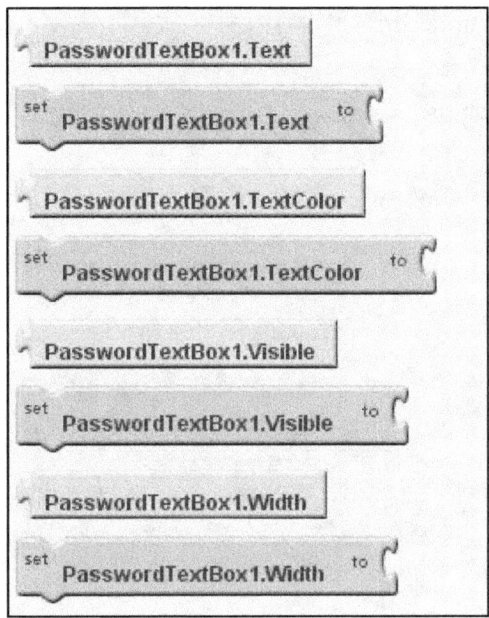

Figure 6.20

Screen

Screen.ErrorOccurred runs the given action when an error occurs.

Screen.Initialize runs the given action when the screen starts.

See Figure 6.21.

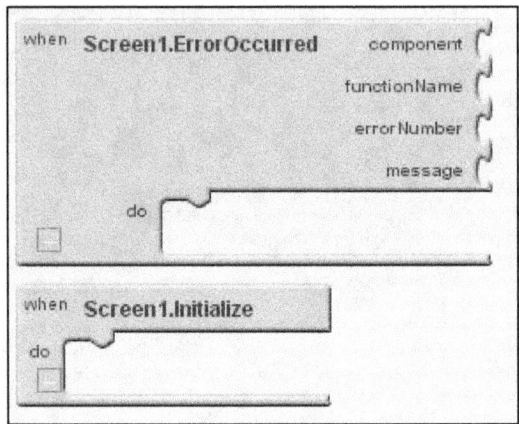

Figure 6.21

The following sets and reports the value of the components property. See Figure 6.22.

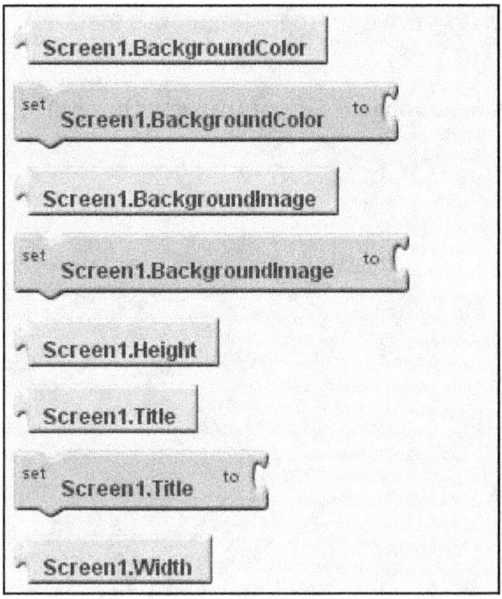

Figure 6.22

TextBox

TextBox.GotFocus starts action when this components is selected for input (textbox is touched).

TextBox.LostFocus starts action when this component is no longer selected for input (different textbox is touched).

See Figure 6.23.

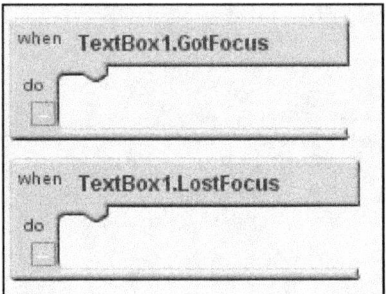

Figure 6.23

124

TextBox.BackgroundColor is the background color of the input box.

TextBox.Enabled determines whether the user can enter text into this box.

TextBox.Height reports the values of the components properties.

TextBox.Hint is text that appears faintly in the input box that provides a password hint.

TextBox.NumbersOnly is a text box that accepts only numbers as keyboard input.

See Figure 6.24.

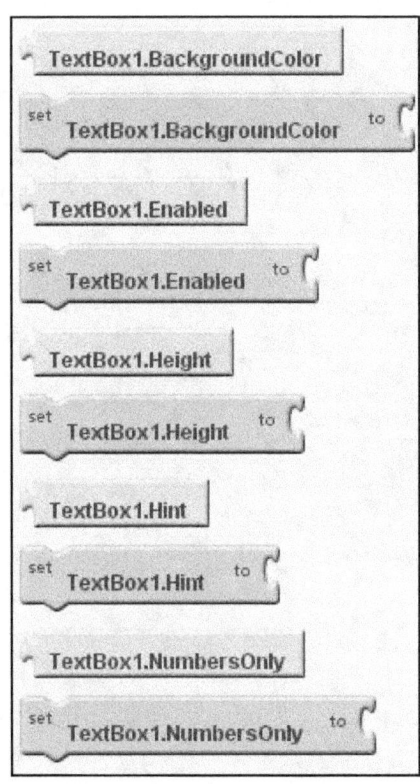

Figure 6.24

125

TextBox.Text is the text in the input box.

TextBox.TextColor is the color of the text.

TextBox.Visible determines if the textbox is visible.

TextBox.Width reports the value of the components property.

See Figure 6.25.

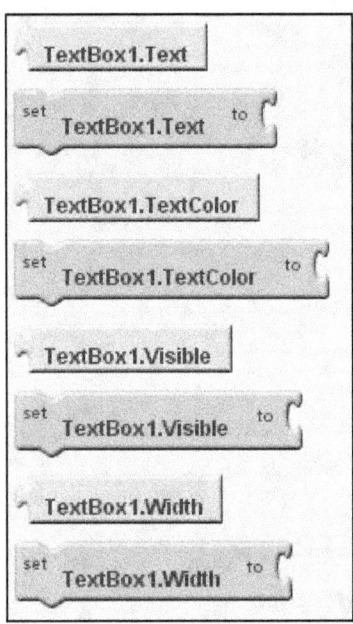

Figure 6.25

TinyDB

TinyDB.GetValue retrieves that given value.

TinyDB.StoreValue stores that given value.

See Figure 6.26.

Figure 6.26

Camera

Camera.AfterPicture is the action after a picture is taken.

Camera.TakePicture is the block for taking a picture.

See Figure 6.27

Figure 6.27

128

ImagePicker

ImagePicker.AfterPicking is the action which occurs after the image picker returns its result.

ImagePicker.BeforePicking is the action which occurs when the component is clicked before the image picker is started.

ImagePicker.GotFocus indicates that the cursor has hovered over the button so it is now possible to click it.

ImagePicker.LostFocus indicates that the cursor has hovered away from the button.

See Figure 6.28

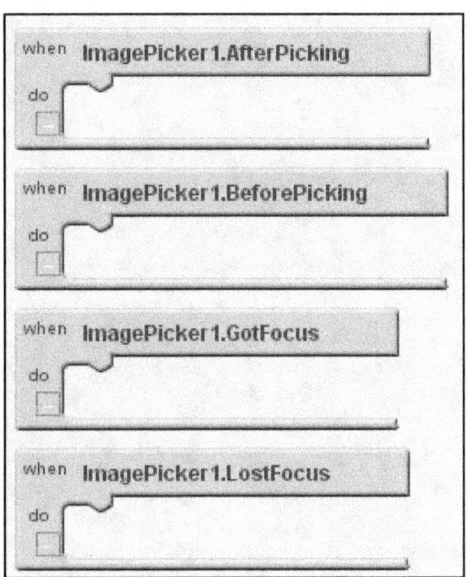

Figure 6.28

The following sets and reports the value of the components property. See Figure 6.29.

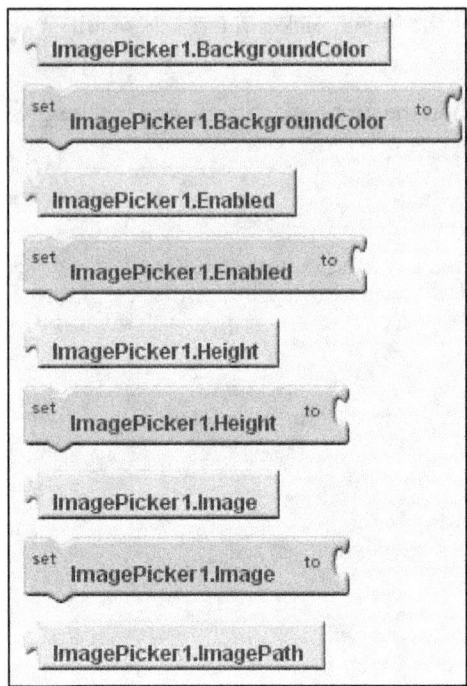

Figure 6.29

The following sets and reports the value of the components property. See Figure 6.30.

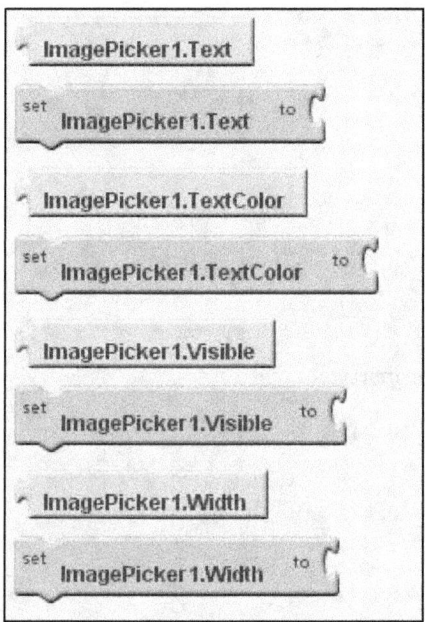

Figure 6.30

Player

Player.Pause pauses the media player if it is playing.

Player.Start starts the media player if it is playing.

Player.Stop stops the media player if it is playing.

Player.Vibrate vibrates for the specified amount of time.

Player.Source sets and reports the value of the components property.

See Figure 6.31.

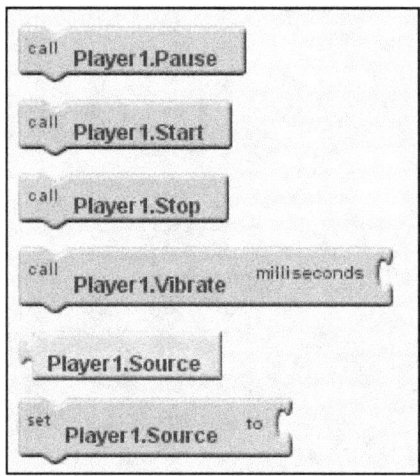

Figure 6.31

Sound

Sound.Pause pauses the sound if it is playing.

Sound.Start starts the sound if it is playing.

Sound.Stop stops the sound if it is playing.

Sound.Vibrate vibrates for the specified amount of time.

See Figure 6.32

Figure 6.32

Sound.MinimumInterval is the minimum interval.

Sound.Source sets and reports the value of the components property.

See Figure 6.33

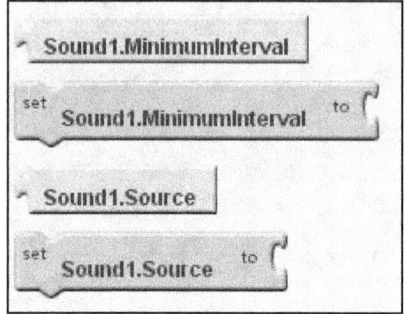

Figure 6.33

VideoPlayer

VideoPlayer.Completed indicates that video player has reached the end.

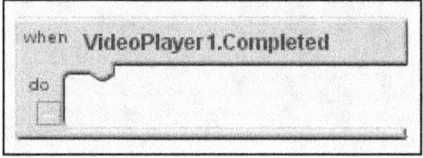

Figure 6.34

VideoPlayer.GetDuration returns the duration of the video.

VideoPlayer.Pause pauses the video.

VideoPlayer.SeekTo seeks to the request time in that video.

VideoPlayer.Start starts the video.

See Figure 6.35.

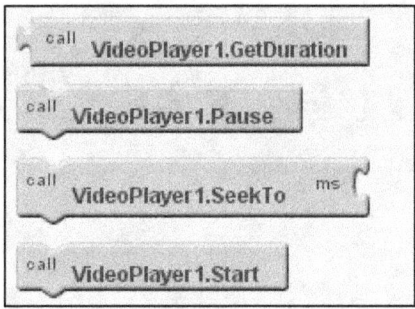

Figure 6.35

135

VideoPlayer.Source is the path to the video.

VideoPlayer.Visible determines if the component is visible.

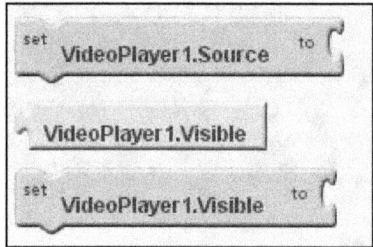

Figure 6.36

ContactPicker

ContactPicker.AfterPicking action occurs after the contact picker activity returns its result.

ContactPicker.BeforePicking action occurs when the component is clicked but before the contact picker activity is started.

ContactPicker.GotFocus indicates the cursor has hovered over the button.

ContactPicker.LostFocus indicates the cursor has hovered away from the button.

See Figure 6.37.

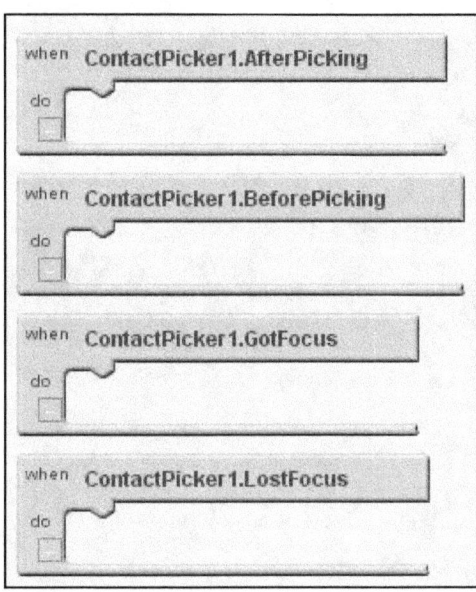

Figure 6.37

The following sets and reports the value of the components property. See Figure 6.38.

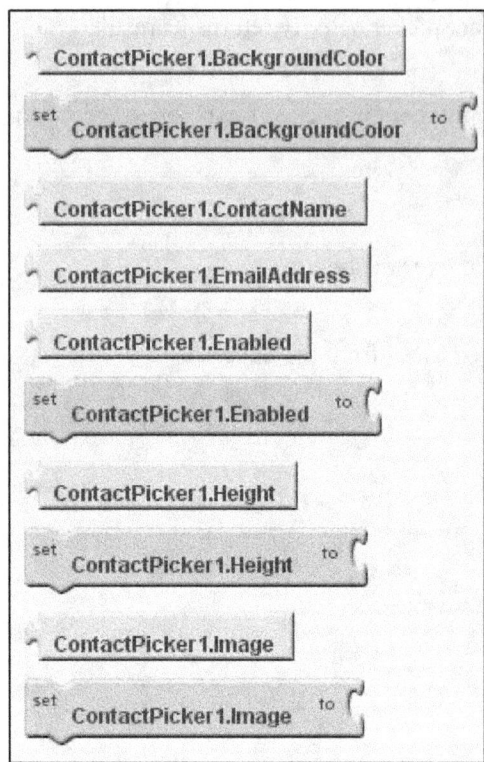

Figure 6.38

The following sets and reports the value of the components property. See Figure 6.39.

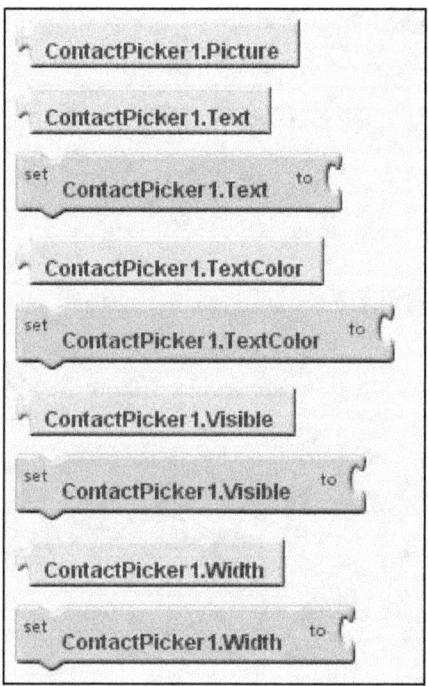

Figure 6.39

139

EmailPicker

EmailPicker.GotFocus activates when this component is selected for input.

EmailPicker.LostFocus activates when this components is no longer selected as input.

See Figure 6.40

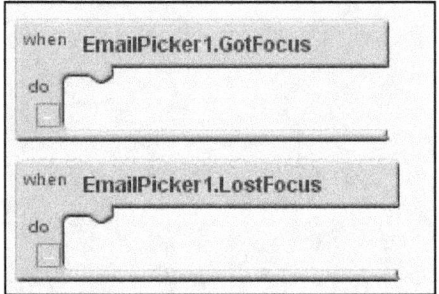

Figure 6.40

EmailPicker.BackgroundColor is the background color of the input box.

EmailPicker.Enabled determines whether the user can enter text into this input box.

EmailPicker.Height sets and records the value of the component property.

EmailPicker.Hint is the grayed out text that appears in the input box to provide a hint.

See Figure 6.41

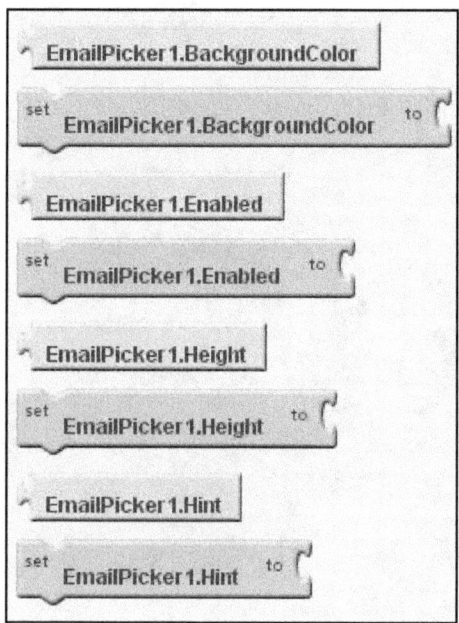

Figure 6.41

EmailPicker.Text is the text in the input box.

EmailPicker.TextColor is the color for the text.

EmailPicker.Visible determines whether the component is visible.

EmailPicker.Width sets and reports the value of the component's property.

See Figure 6.42

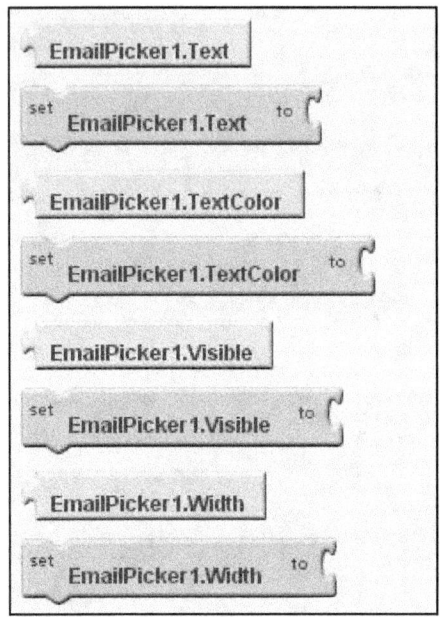

Figure 6.42

PhoneCall

PhoneCall.MakePhoneCall is the block for making a phone call.

PhoneCall.PhoneNumber sets and reports the value of the component property.

See Figure 6.43

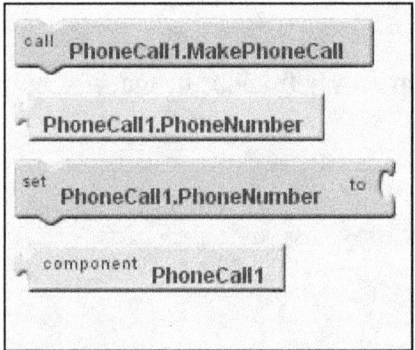

Figure 6.43

PhoneNumberPicker

PhoneNumberPicker.AfterPicking action occurs after the contact picker returns its result.

PhoneNumberPicker.BeforePicking action occurs when the component is clicked but before the contact picker activity is started.

PhoneNumberPicker.GotFocus indicates that the cursor hovered over the button.

PhoneNumberPicker.LostFocus indicates that the cursor hovered away from the button.

See Figure 6.44.

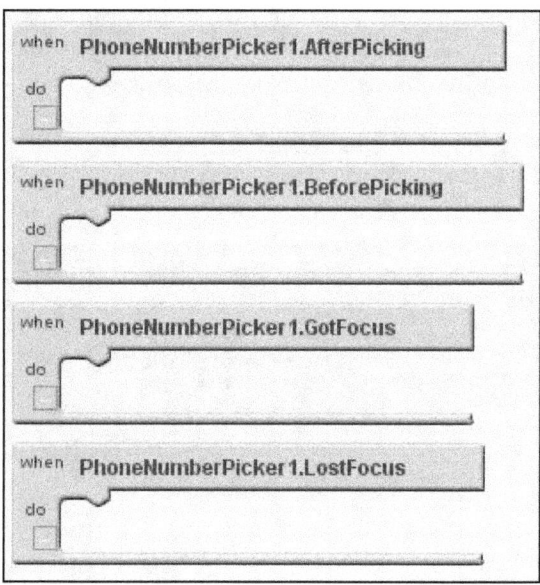

Figure 6.44

144

The following sets and reports the value of the components property. See Figure 6.45.

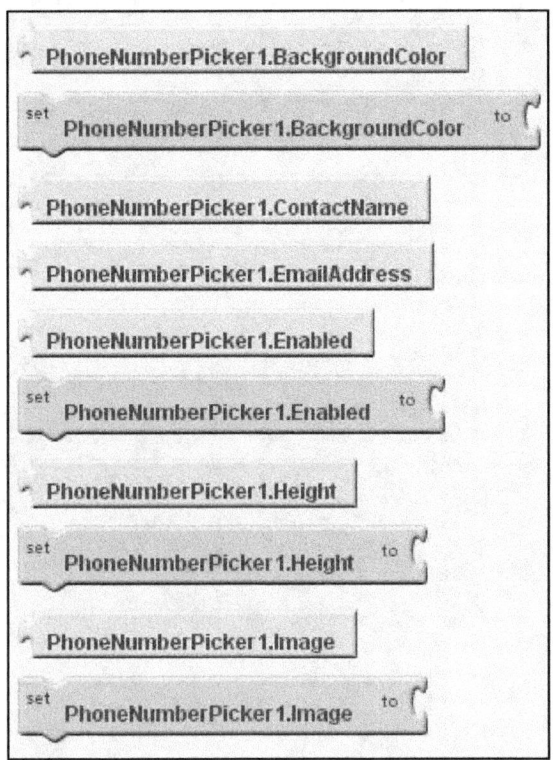

Figure 6.45

The following sets and reports the value of the components property. See Figure 6.46.

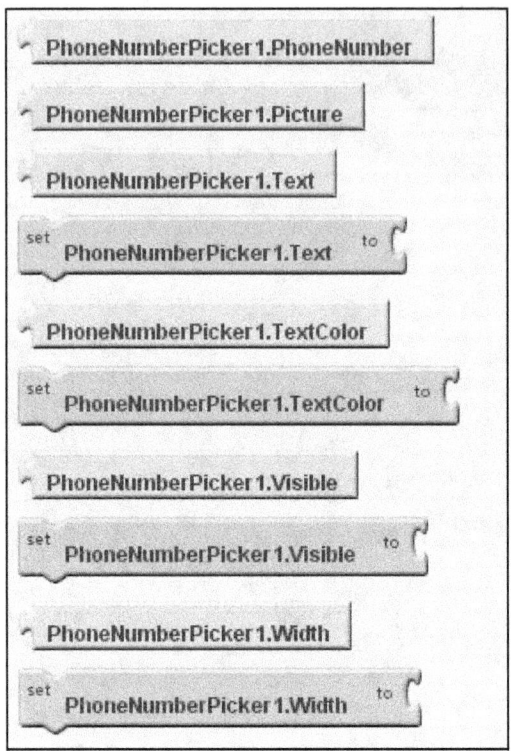

Figure 6.46

Texting

Texting.MessageReceived action occurs when a new text message is received by the phone.

Texting.SendMessage sends a text message.

Texting.PhoneNumber sets and reports the value of the component's property.

Texting.ReceivingEnabled sets and reports the value of the component's property.

See Figure 6.47.

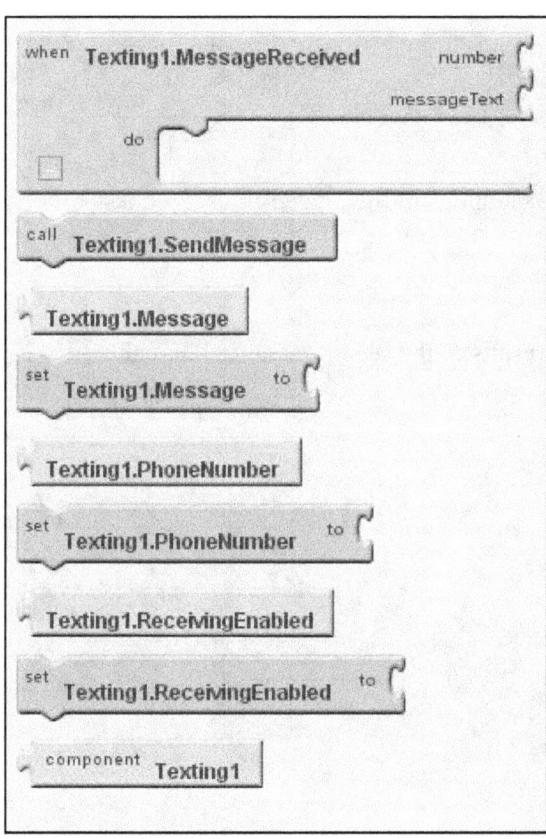

Figure 6.47

147

Twitter

Twitter.DirectMessageReceived action occurs when the recent messages requested through RequestDirectMessages have been received.

Twitter.FollowersReceived action occurs when all of the followers of the logged in user requested though RequestFollowers have been retrieved.

Twitter.FriendTimelineReceived action occurs when the messages requested though RequestFriendTimeline have been retrieved.

Twitter.IsAuthorized action occurs when the program calls Authorize if authorization was successful.

Twitter.MentionsReceived action occurs when the mentions of the logged-in user requested through RequestMentions have been retrieved.

Twitter.SearchSuccessful action occurs when the results of the search requested though SearchSuccesful have been retrieved.

See Figure 6.48.

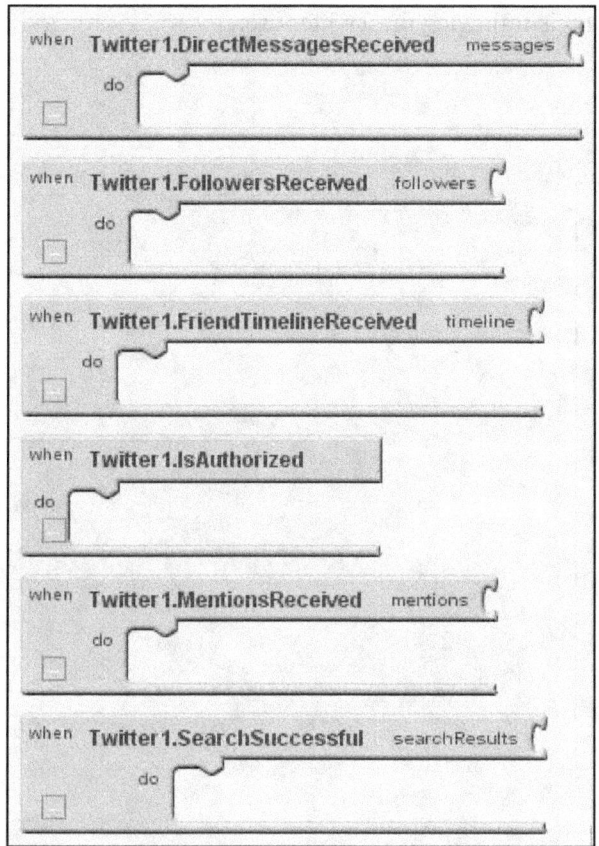

Figure 6.48

Twitter.Authrorize redirects user to login to Twitter via the web browser.

Twitter.CheckAuthorized checks if access has been granted.

Twitter.DeAuthorize removes Twitter authorization from this instance of the application.

Twitter.DirectMessage sends a direct private message to the specified user.

Twitter.Follow starts following a user.

Twitter.RequestDirectMessages requests the most recent 20 direct messages sent to the Twitter user.

Twitter.RequestFollowers retrieves a list of who is following the Twitter user.

See Figure 6.49.

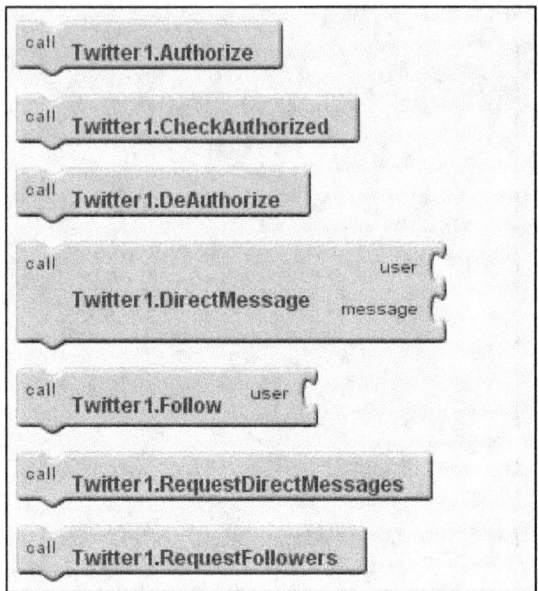

Figure 6.49

Twitter.RequestFriendTimeline gets 20 of the most recent messages of users that follow the Twitter user.

Twitter.RequestMentions requests the most 20 recent mentions of the Twitter user.

Twitter.SearchTwitter searches for tweets or labels.

Twitter.SetStatus updates the Twitter user's status to the specified text.

Twitter.StopFollowing stops following a user.

See Figure 6.50

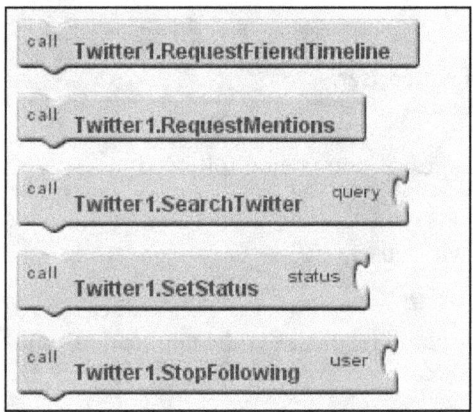

Figure 6.50

The following sets and reports the value of the components property. See Figure 6.51.

Figure 6.51

Twitter.DirectMessages contains a list of the most recent message mentioning the Twitter user.

Twitter.Followers contains a list of the followers of the Twitter user.

Twitter.FriendTimeline contains the most recent 20 messages of users being followed.

Twitter.Mentions contains a list of the mentions of the Twitter user.

Twitter.SearchResults is initially empty, is set to a list of search results after the application runs the SearchTwitter block.

Twitter.Username is the user name of the authorized user.

See Figure 6.52.

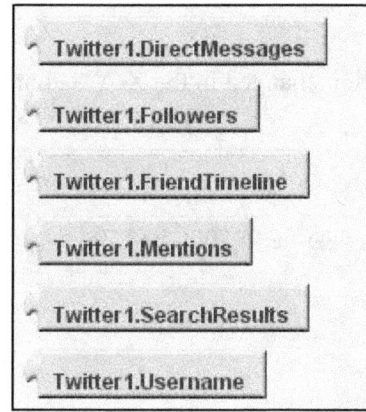

Figure 6.52

AccelerometerSensor

AccelerometerSensor.AccelerationChanged indicates the acceleration changed in the X, Y and or Z dimensions.

AccelerometerSensor.Shaking indicates that the device has started shaking or continues to be shaken.

See Figure 6.53.

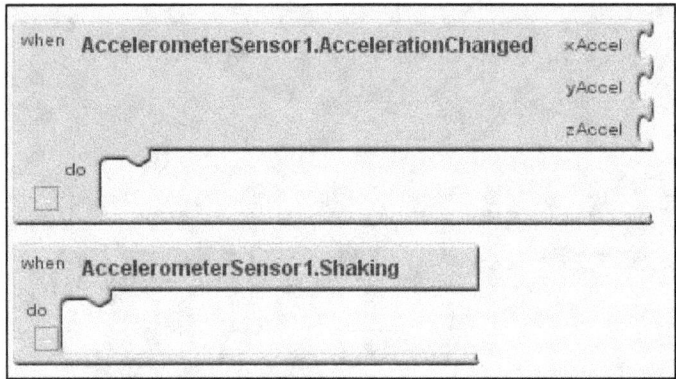

Figure 6.53

The following sets and reports the value of the component's property. See Figure 6.54.

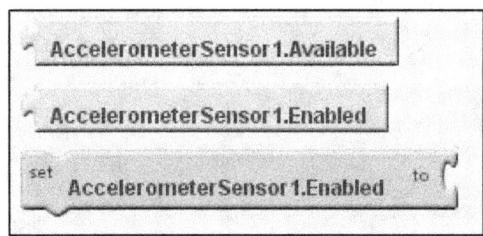

Figure 6.54

154

The following sets and reports the value of the component's property. See Figure 6.55.

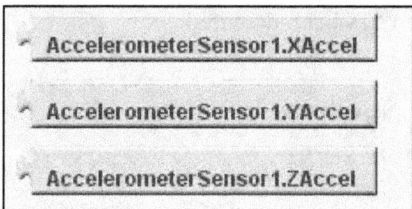

Figure 6.55

LocationSensor

LocationSensor.LocationChanged indicates that a new location has been detected.

LocationSensor.StatusChanged indicates that the status of the provider has changed.

See Figure 6.56.

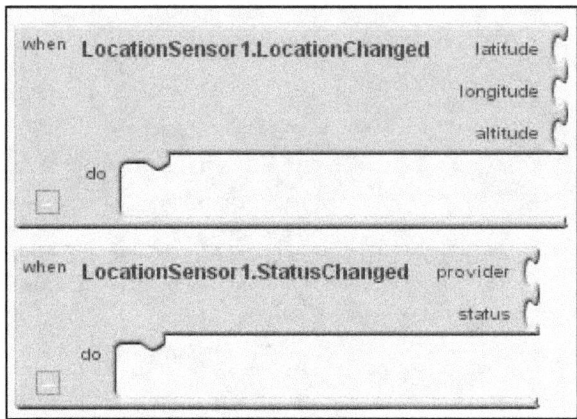

Figure 6.56

LocationSensor.LatitudeFromAddress gets latitude of a given address.

LocationSensor.LongitudeFromAddress gets longitude of a given address.

See Figure 6.57.

Figure 6.57

156

The following sets and reports the value of the component's property. See Figure 6.58.

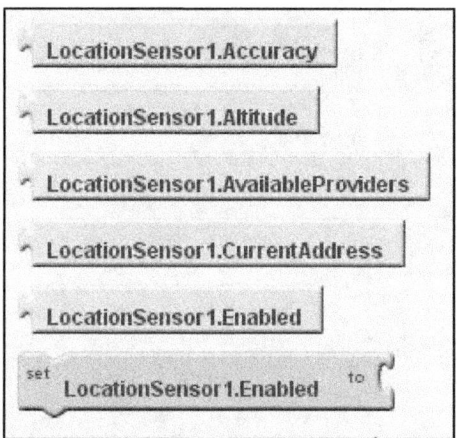

Figure 6.58

The following sets and reports the value of the component's property. See Figure 6.59.

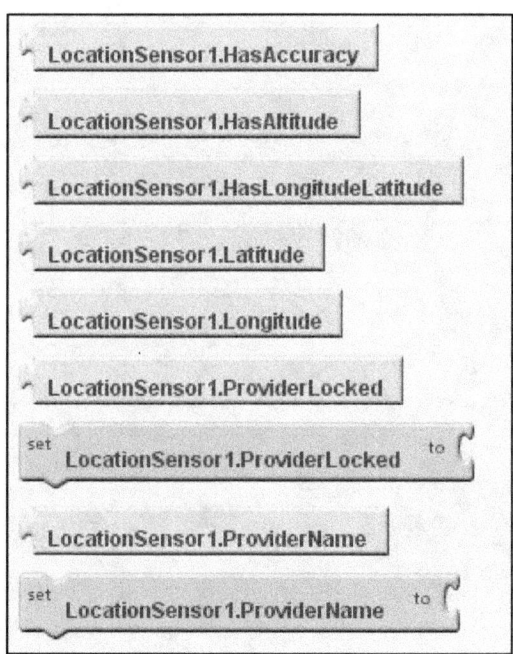

Figure 6.59

OrientationSensor

OrientationSensor.OrientationChanged occurs when the device's orientation has changed. See Figure 6.60.

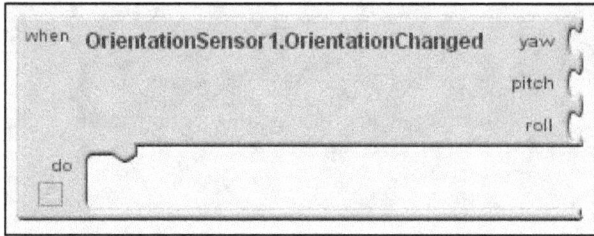

Figure 6.60

The following sets and reports the value of the component's property. See Figure 6.61.

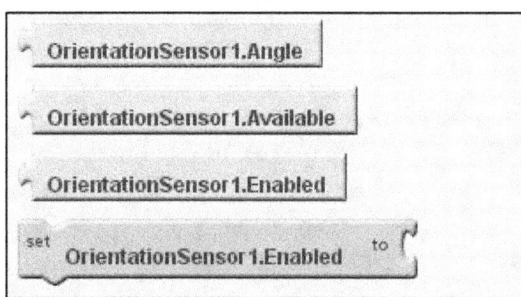

Figure 6.61

The following sets and reports the value of the component's property. See Figure 6.62.

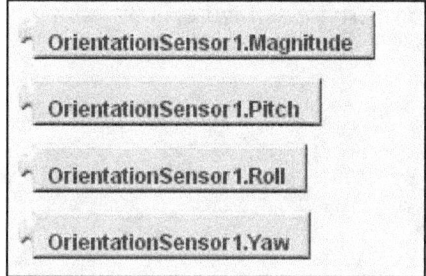

Figure 6.62

HorizontalArrangement

The following sets and reports the value of the component's property. See Figure 6.63.

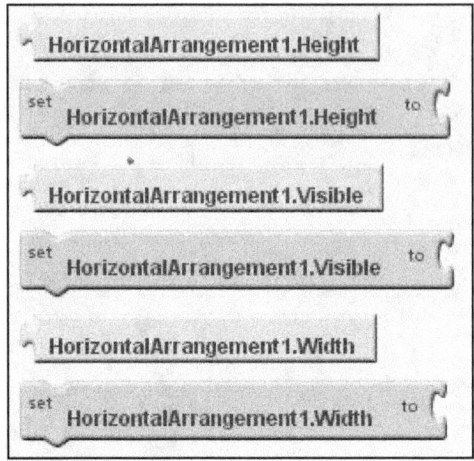

Figure 6.63

TableArrangement

The following sets and reports the value of the component's property. See Figure 6.64.

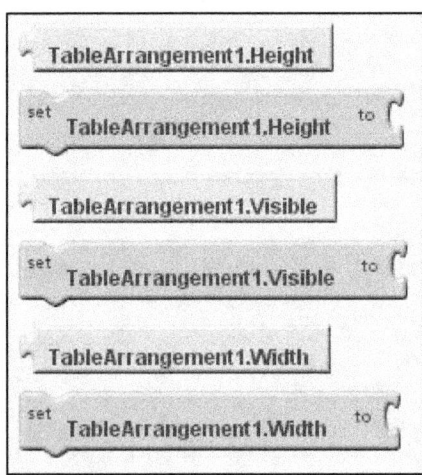

Figure 6.64

VerticalArrangement

The following sets and reports the value of the component's property. See Figure 6.65.

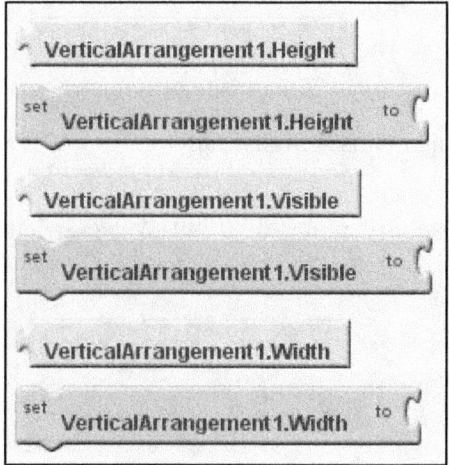

Figure 6.65

ActivityStarter

ActivityStarter.AfterActivity occurs after result returns.

ActivityStarter.ResolveActivity returns the name of the activity that corresponds to this ActivityStarter.

ActivityStarter.StartActivity starts the activity corresponding to this ActivityStarter.

ActivityStarter.Action, ActivityStarter.ActivityClass and ActivityStarter.ActivityPackage set and report the value of the component property.

See Figure 6.66.

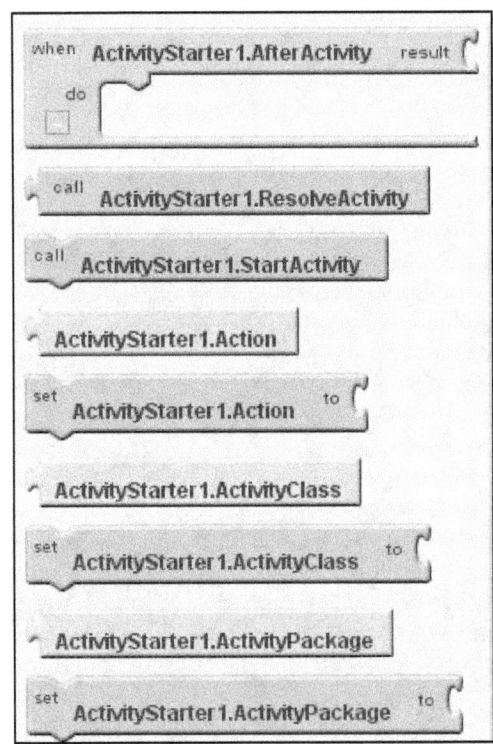

Figure 6.66

162

The following sets and reports the value of the component's property. See Figure 6.67.

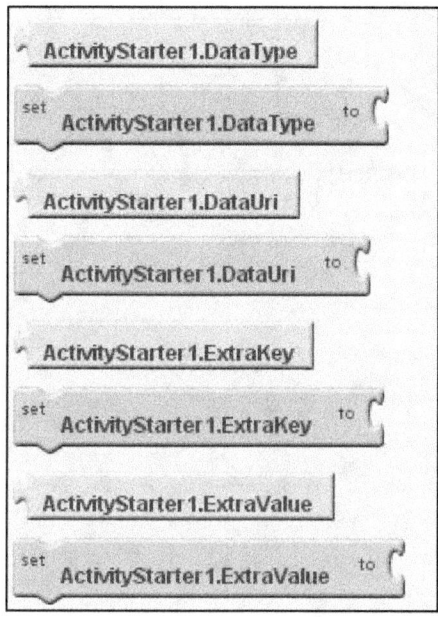

Figure 6.67

The following sets and reports the value of the component's property. See Figure 6.68.

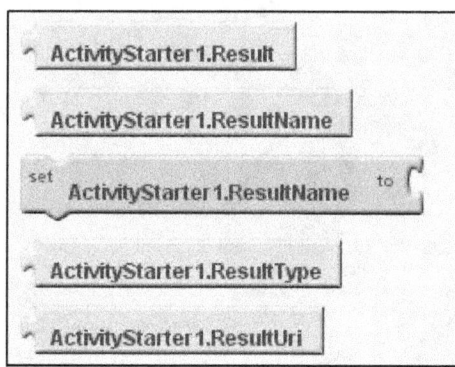

Figure 6.68

BarcodeScanner

BarcodeScanner.AfterScan occurs after the scanner activity has returned.

BarcodeScanner.DoScan is the block for DoScan.

BarcodeScanner.Result reports the value of the component's property.

See Figure 6.69

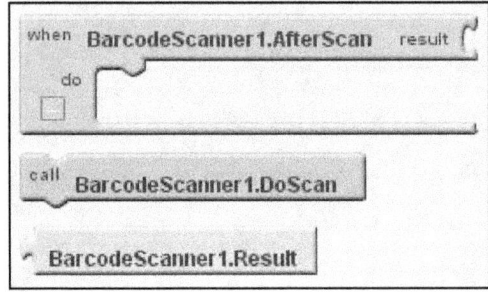

Figure 6.69

Notifier

Notifier.AfterChoosing occurs after the user has made a selection for ShowChooseDialog.

Notifier.AfterTextInput occurs after the user has responded to ShowTextDialog.

See Figure 6.70.

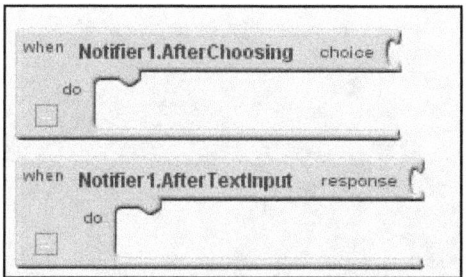

Figure 6.70

Notifier.LogError, Notifier.LogInfo and Notifier.LogWarning are for logging information messages.

Notifier.ShowAlert displays a temporary notification.

See Figure 6.71.

Figure 6.71

Notifier.ShowChooseDialog displays an alert with 2 buttons.

Notifier .ShowMessageDialog displays an alert with 1 button.

Notifier .ShowTextDialog is the notifier block for showing the text dialog.

See Figure 6.72.

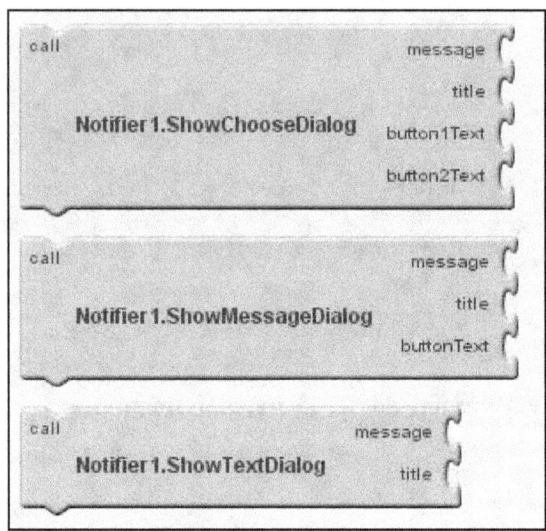

Figure 6.72

SpeechRecognizer

SpeechRecognizer.AfterGettingText occurs after getting input.

SpeechRecognizer.BeforeGettingText occurs before getting input.

SpeechRecognizer.GetText is the action for getting text.

SpeechRecognizer.Result reports the value of the component's property.

See Figure 6.73.

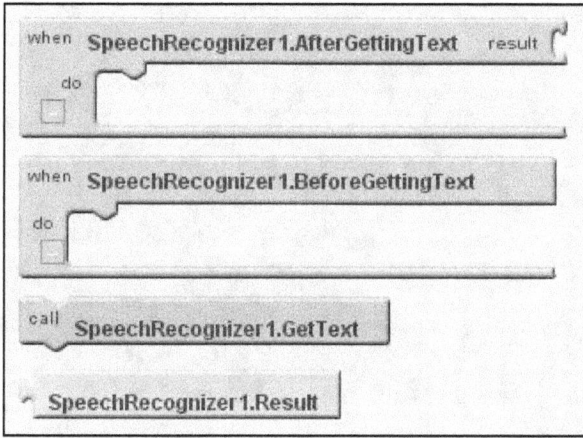

Figure 6.73

TextToSpeech

TextToSpeech.AfterSpeaking occurs after the message is spoken.

TextToSpeech.BeforeSpeaking occurs before the message is spoken.

TextToSpeech.Speak is the block for speak.

TextToSpeech.Country, TextToSpeech.Language and TextToSpeech.Result set and report the value of the component's property.

See Figure 6.74.

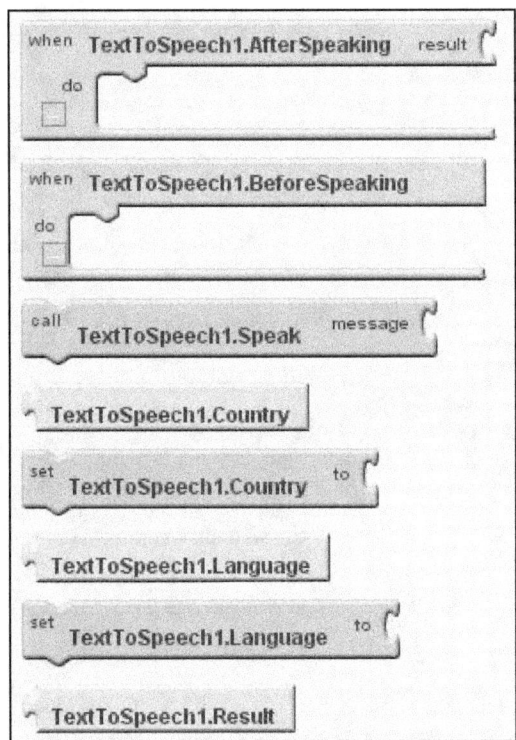

Figure 6.74

There is a lot of information in the My Blocks section. Remember, Blocks Editor will only show blocks when you have added the corresponding component in Designer. Thus, your blocks are based on selections that you determine in Designer. As stated earlier in this book, the Blocks Editor is like our "instructions" for our recipe. In the later chapters we will build our 1st application and examine many other applications.

Your 1st

Application

"Hello World"

The Recipe

Building an application with App Inventor is like cooking food by following a recipe. For those of you who cook, you know that there are 2 main parts to any recipe. These 2 parts are:

1) The Ingredients

2) The Instructions

Using the Designer is like making a list of and assembling the ingredients.

Using the Blocks Editor is like creating and following the instructions.

Hello World

In this chapter we will create our 1st Android App Inventor application called "Hello World". This application will be a simple image that will play a sound when clicked. Before we begin visit http://android-apps-development.com/home/apps-download/ and download the file named Hello_World.zip. This file contains 2 files (diddy.jpg and hello.wav) that we need for our "Hello World" app. Unzip the zip file. Next, we start the process by opening App Inventor Designer and creating a new project. We click New. See Figure 7.1.

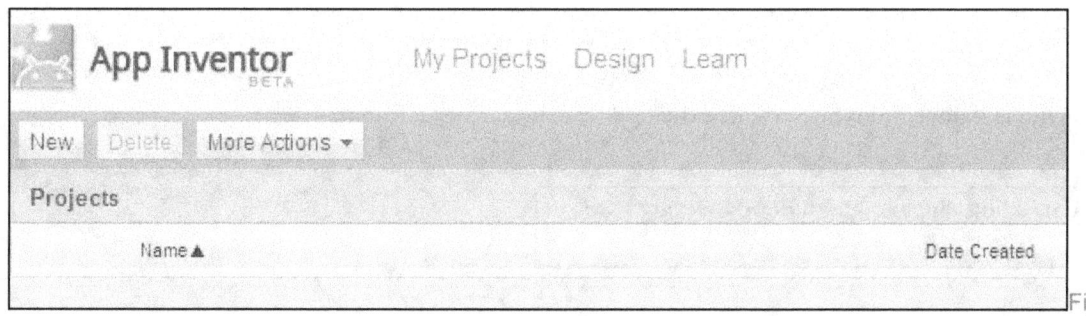

Figure 7.1

Next, we name our project "Hello_World". App Inventor does not allow for spaces in project names. See Figure 7.2.

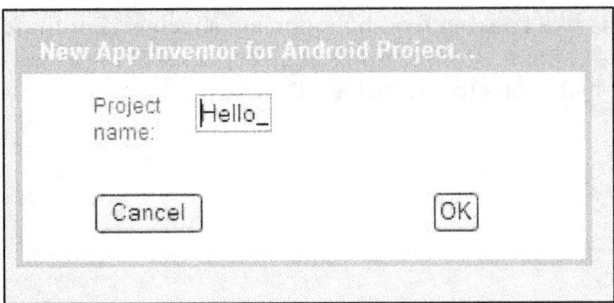

Figure 7.2

Next, we want to add media. We will be adding an image and a sound file. Click Add. See Figure 7.3.

Figure 7.3

Next, we browse to select the media file then we click OK. See Figure 7.4.

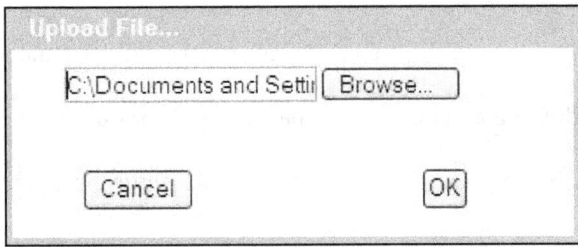

Figure 7.4

Our file is named diddy.jpg. Notice the update message. See Figure 7.5.

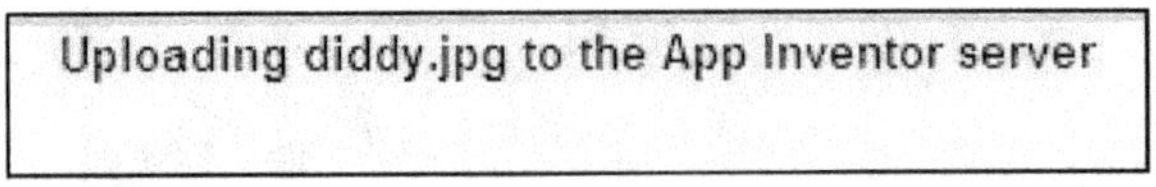

Uploading diddy.jpg to the App Inventor server

Figure 7.5

Next, we upload our sound file named hello.wav. Notice the update message. See Figure 7.7.

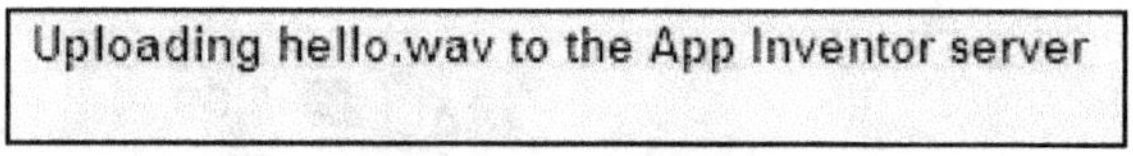
Uploading hello.wav to the App Inventor server

Figure 7.6

Notice our media files have been uploaded and are listed in the media section. See Figure 7.7.

Media
diddy.jpg
hello.wav
Add...

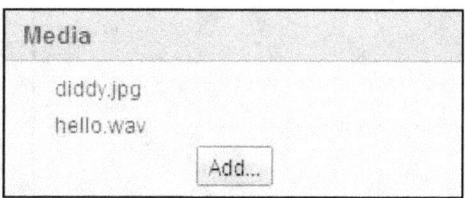

Figure 7.7

Our application will play a sound when clicked, so we will need to add a button which allows for events to happen. Next, drag and drop Button onto Screen1. See Figure 7.8.

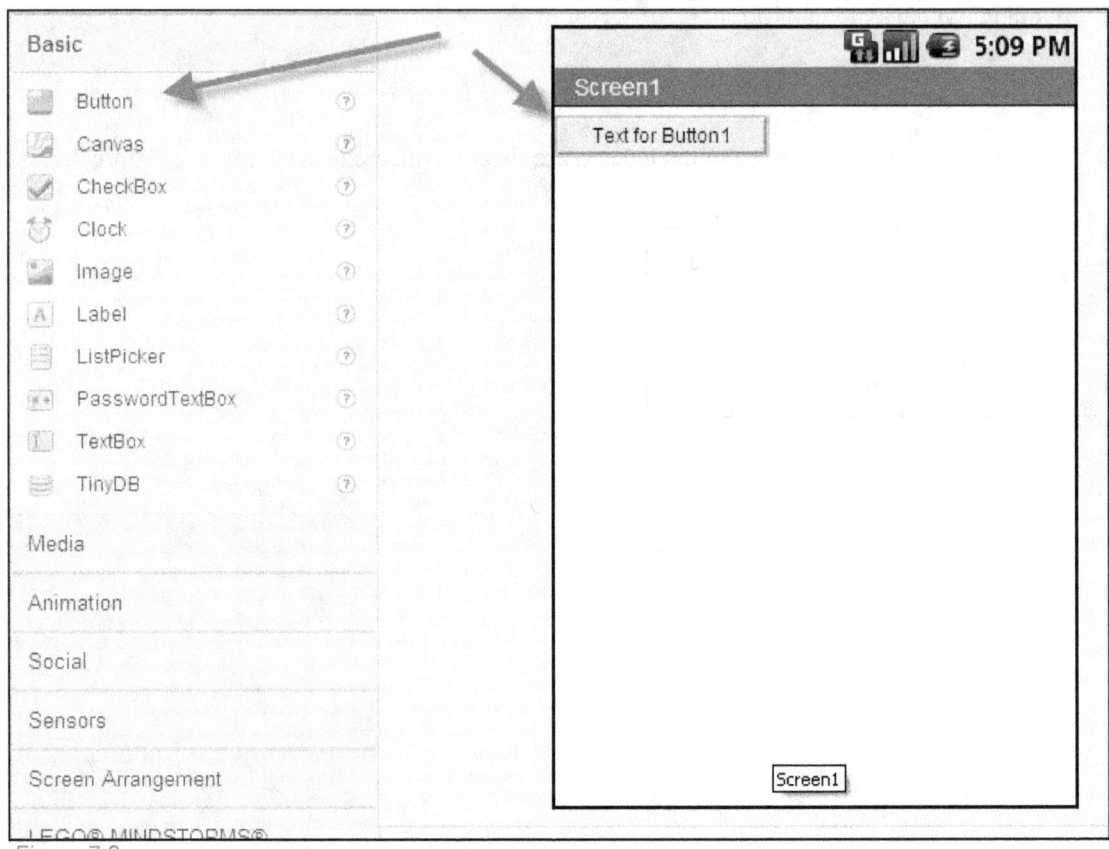

Figure 7.8

After you drag and drop, click "Text for Button1". Clicking on "Text for Button1" will reveal configuration options for Button. See Figure 7.9.

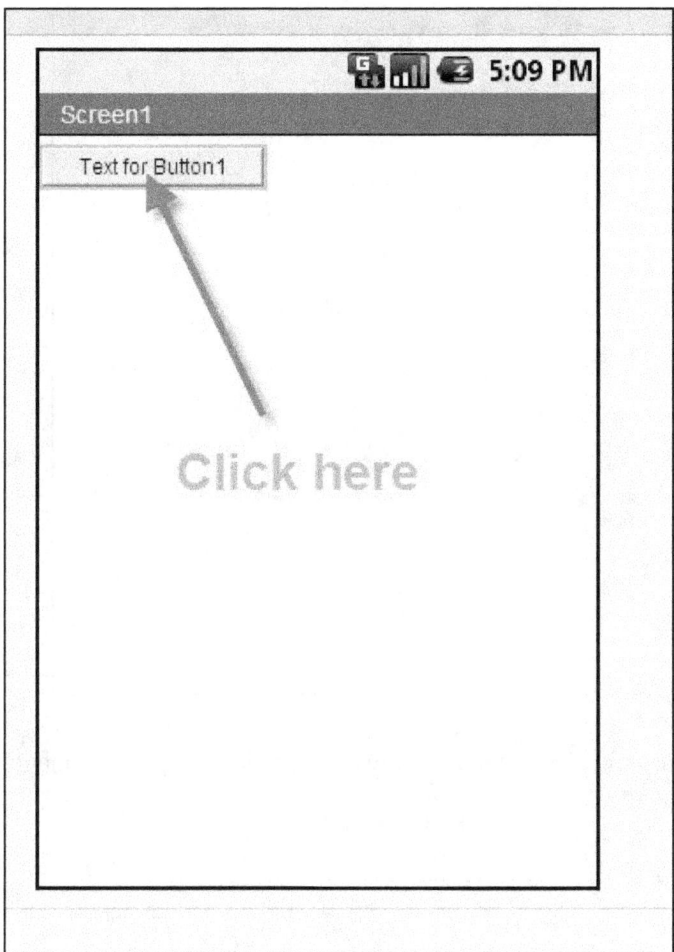

Figure 7.9

We want an image to be our "button". Currently, there is no image associated with the Button. In Figure 7.10, under Properties, under Image the word None is listed. Click None.

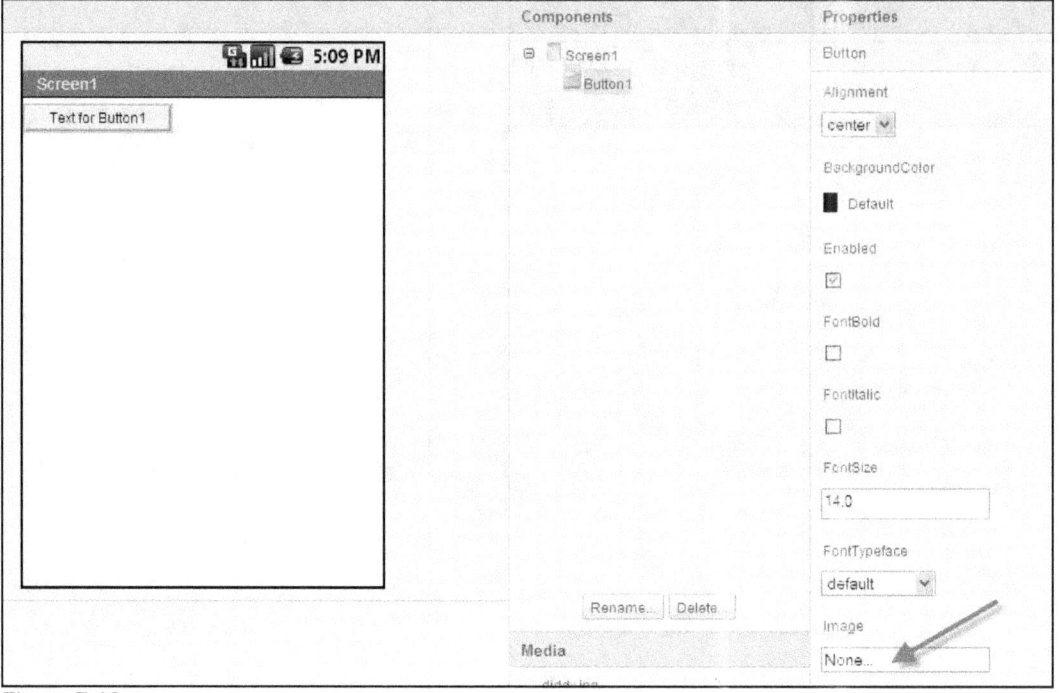

Figure 7.10

Designer allows you to select from your uploaded media. Next we select diddy.jpg as our image.

See Figure 7.11.

Figure 7.11

The default width and height are set to automatic. See Figure 7.12.

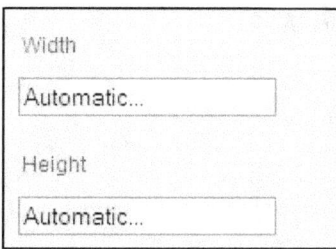

Figure 7.12

Notice that our button image is not visible. See Figure 7.13. We will have to specify the dimensions in pixels.

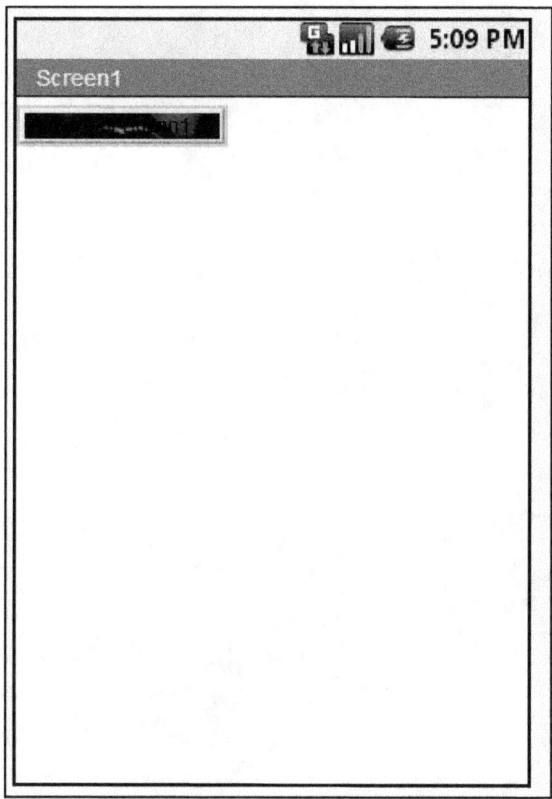

Figure 7.13

177

We set the width and height to 300 pixels. See Figure 7.14 and Figure 7.15.

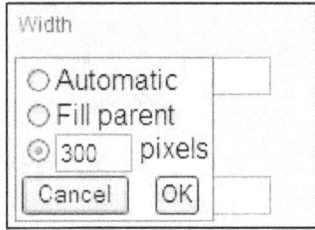

Figure 7.14

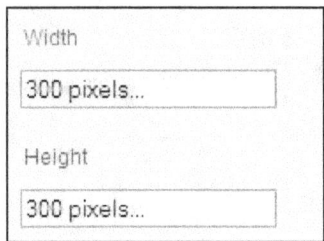

Figure 7.15

Notice the results of the dimensions change. See Figure 7.16.

Figure 7.16

Next, we want to change the text color on the button from black to white. We do this by clicking TextColor and selecting White from the list of colors.

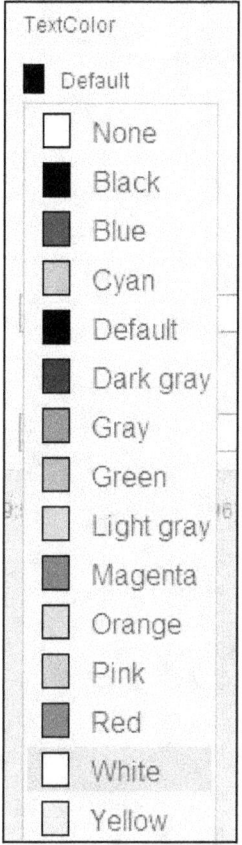

Figure 7.17

Next, we change the font size to 25 by changing the FontSize setting. See Figure 7.18.

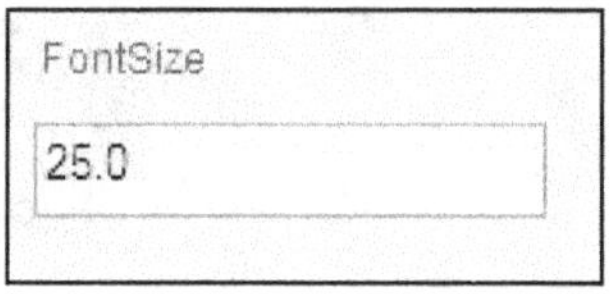

FontSize

25.0

Figure 7.18

We want the text on the button to say "Hello World" so we add "Hello World" to the Text field. See Figure 7.19.

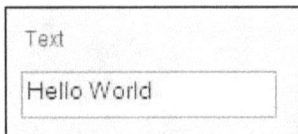

Figure 7.19

Notice the results of our changes in Figure 7.20.

Figure 7.20

180

Next, we want to create a label to accompany our button. Drag and drop Label to Screen1. See Figure 7.21.

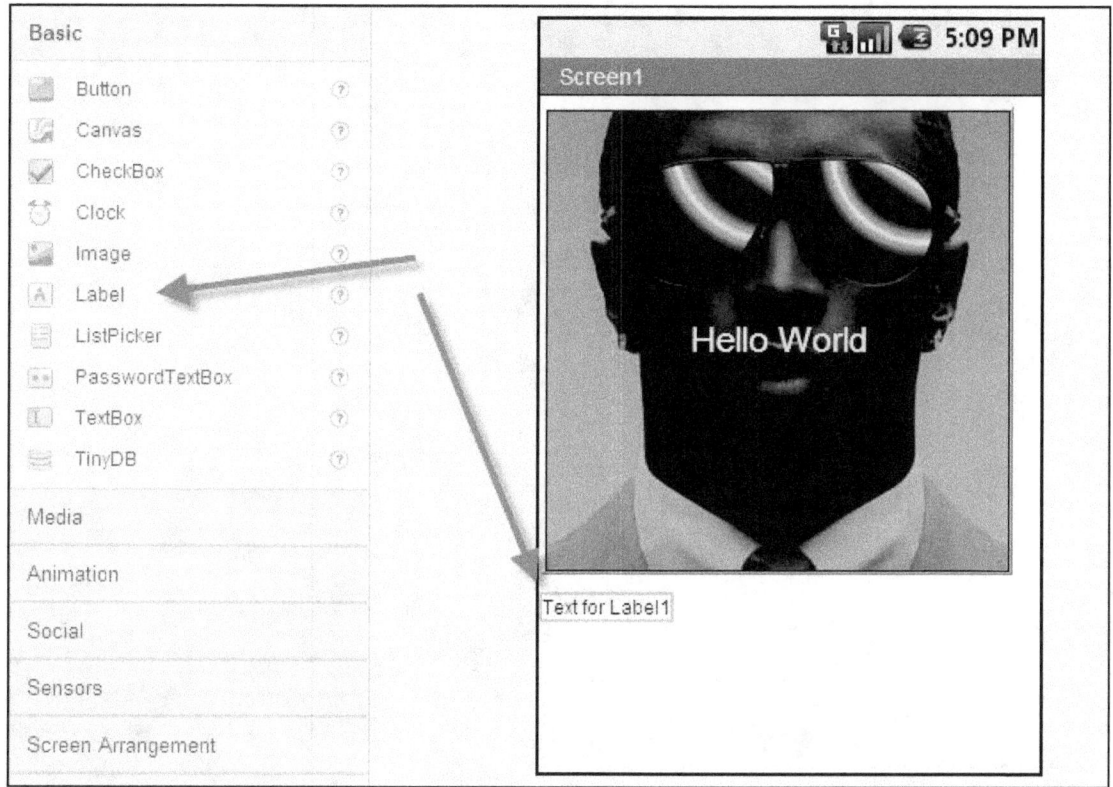

Figure 7.21

Next, we want to configure Label. We click on Label and change FontSize to 25.0, we check FontBold and add "Hello, Good Morning" to the Text field. See Figure 7.22.

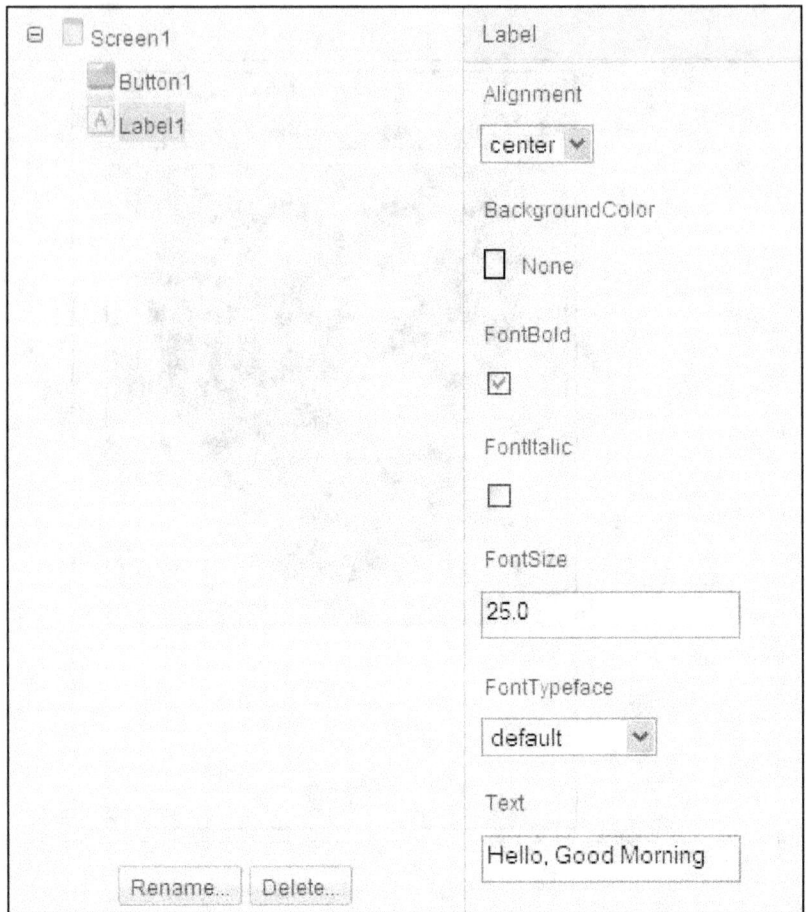

Figure 7.22

See the results of our changes in Figure 7.23.

Figure 7.23

Next, we want to add sound to our application. Drag and drop Sound to Screen1. See Figure 7.24.

Figure 7.24

Next, click Sound1 and change the source from None to hello.wav. See Figure 7.25.

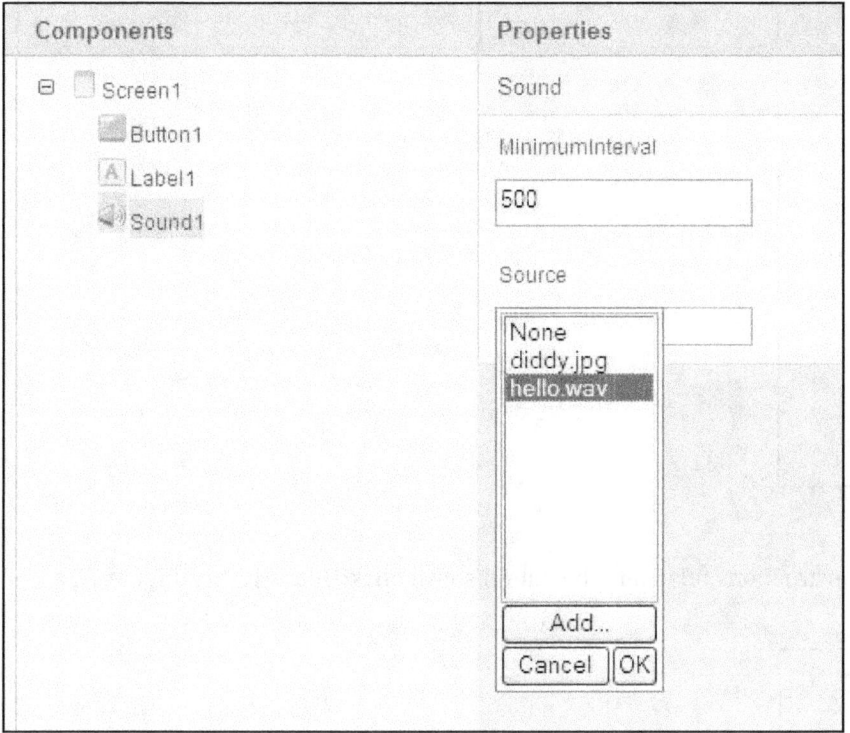

Figure 7.25

We have finished designing our application in Designer. Our ingredients have been prepared.

Next we want to create/follow the instructions so we launch the Blocks Editor. See Figure 7.26

Figure 7.26

Next, we click "My Blocks". See Figure 7.27.

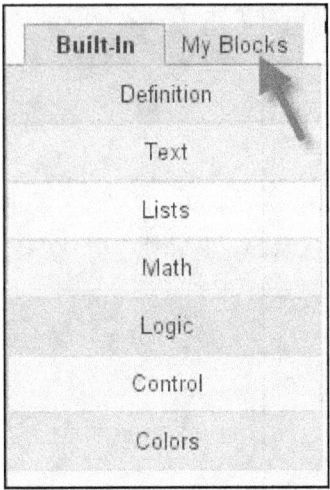

Figure 7.27

Next, we want to give instructions related to the button so we click Button1. See Figure 7.28.

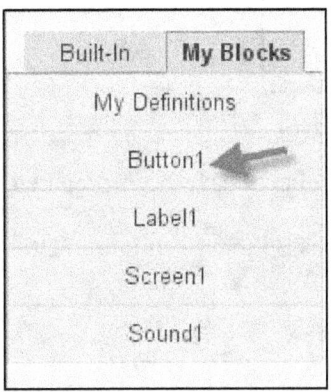

Figure 7.28

We want something to happen when the button is clicked. So, we click the block titled Button1.Click. Notice the "when" and "do". This simply means, when the button is click do something. See Figure 7.29.

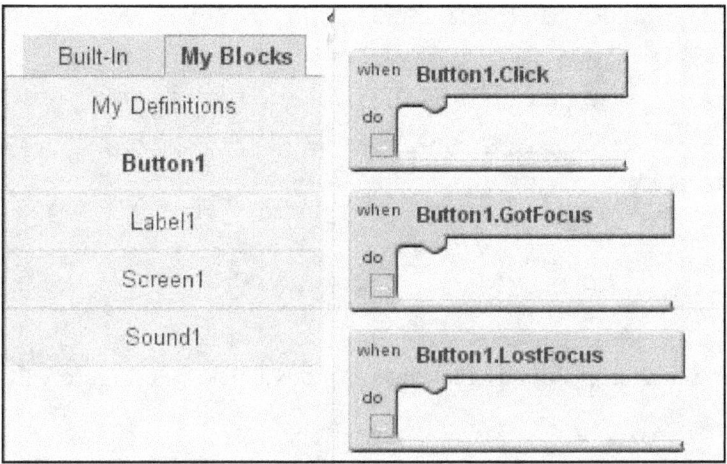

Figure 7.29

Next, drag and drop Button1.Click to the main blocks area. See Figure 7.30.

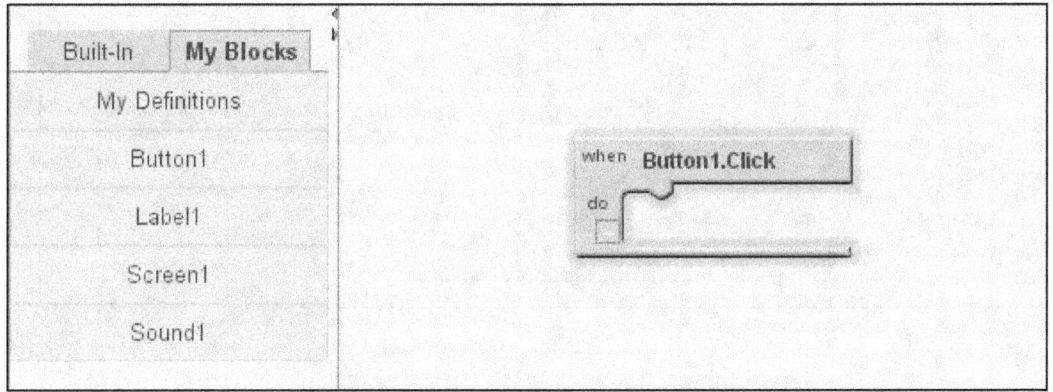

Figure 7.30

Next, we want to add sound. Click on Sound1. See Figure 7.31.

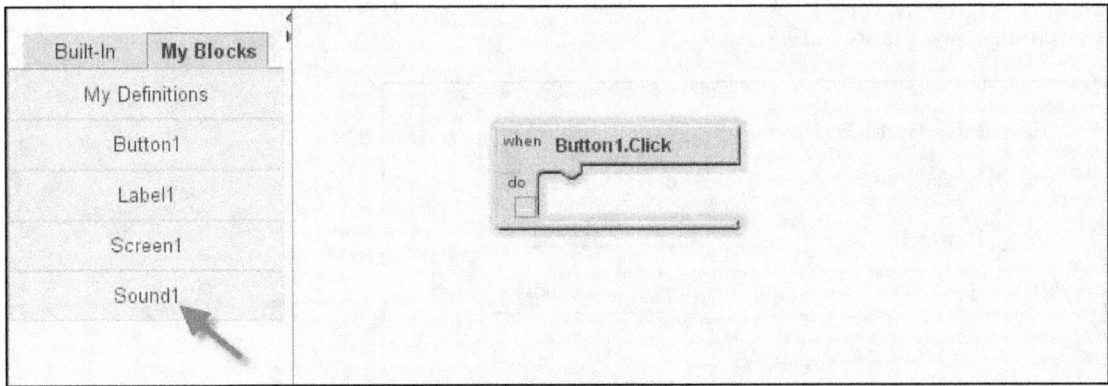

Figure 7.31

We want the sound to play so drag and drop Sound1.Play into Button1.Click. See Figure 7.32

and Figure 7.33.

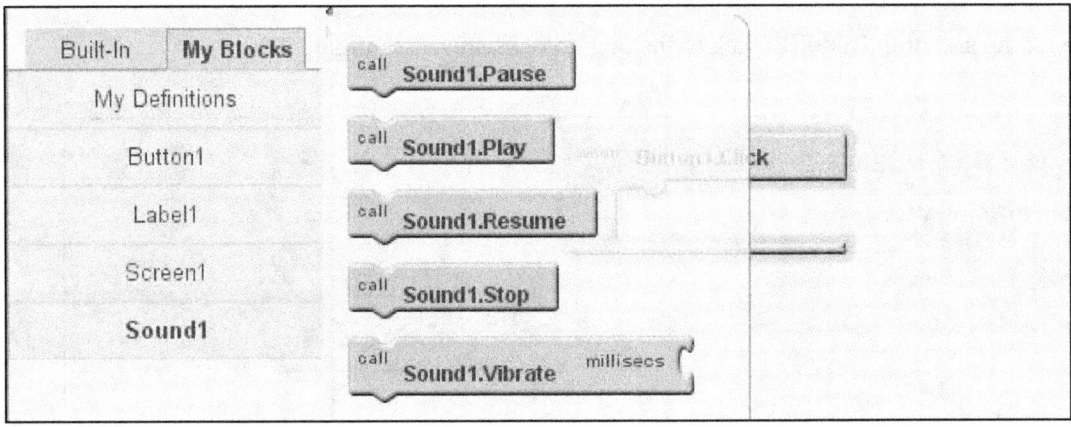

Figure 7.32

Figure 7.33

You can have your application run in the emulator or run on your Android phone. For all of the demonstrations, I will be using the emulator.

Next, click "Connect to device". See Figure 7.34.

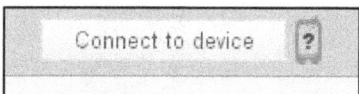

Figure 7.34

Next, click on Diddy's face to hear the "Hello" message. See Figure 7.35.

Figure 7.35

In this chapter we created our 1st App Inventor application. We talked about the recipe concept of having ingredients and instructions. We effectively used the App Inventor Designer and the App Inventor Blocks Editor. I encourage you to experiment with other components of Designer and Block Editor specifically buttons, sound and images. In later chapters we will be creating more complicated applications.

QR Codes

What are QR Codes?

QR codes are barcodes and sometimes referred to as two-dimensional barcodes. QR codes can be read by dedicated QR barcode readers and by camera phones. QR codes are made up of black rectangular boxes which can be used store URLs, text or other data. QR is short for Quick Response as the inventor designed QR codes for speed. QR codes were originally created in Japan by Denso-Wave (a subsidiary of Toyota) in 1994. [11]

Download QR Droid

QR codes allow us to easily access URLs to download and install App Inventor applications on our devices. In the next few chapters, you will be required to download applications using the QR codes. Before we can read QR codes we will need to download QR Droid on our devices. You can begin this process by accessing Market on your device. See Figure 8.1

Figure 8.1

Next, search for QR Droid.

Download QR Droid which is free.

Your device will automatically install the download.

Try QR Droid

Next, locate and open QR Droid on your device.

We will want to scan a QR code with our camera so click "From camera". See Figure 8.2.

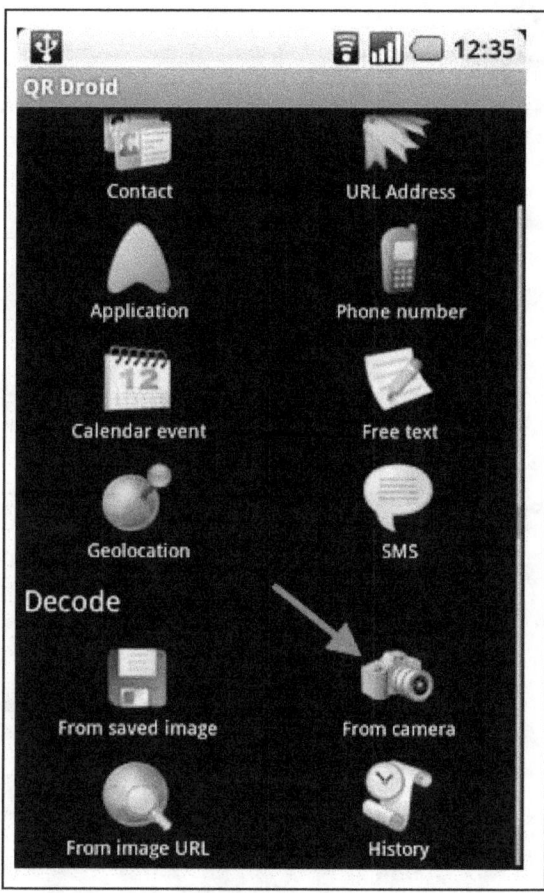

Figure 8.2

In Figure 8.3 we have a QR code. Try scanning it with QR Droid. The result should be a URL (http://thewebacademy.org).

Figure 8.3

We will be scanning more QR codes in the next chapter. For now, practice scanning QR codes

from the web and making QR codes at your leisure.

Your 2nd Application

"PicCall"

For the Hello World application, we built the application from scratch using the App Inventor Designer and Blocks Editor. Moving forward we will be downloading and running applications and examining the source on Designer and Blocks Editor.

PicCall on Our Device

We can download the application directly to our device by scanning the QR code. When we do this, we will NOT be able to edit the application. If you followed the steps in the previous chapter and installed QR Droid then let's download the application. If not, please visit the chapter on QR codes.

Scan the QR code. See Figure 9.1.

Figure 9.1

Follow the steps below:

1) Open the QR Droid application on your device.

2) Next, under Decode, click "From camera".

3) Next, line up the scanner with the QR code.

4) Next, the URL for the application will appear.

5) Click "Open" to open the URL.

6) Next, your device will download the application. We will need to install the application.

7) Next, navigate to the location of your applications.

8) Next click Files, click Download then click PicCall.

9) After installation, open PicCall.

Notice that when you click "Press to Call", nothing happens.

Why is that? We will find out.

PicCall in App Inventor

Next, we will download the PicCall App Inventor source.

Visit the following URL: http://android-apps-development.com/home/apps-download/

Next, click "PicCall Application". See Figure 9.2.

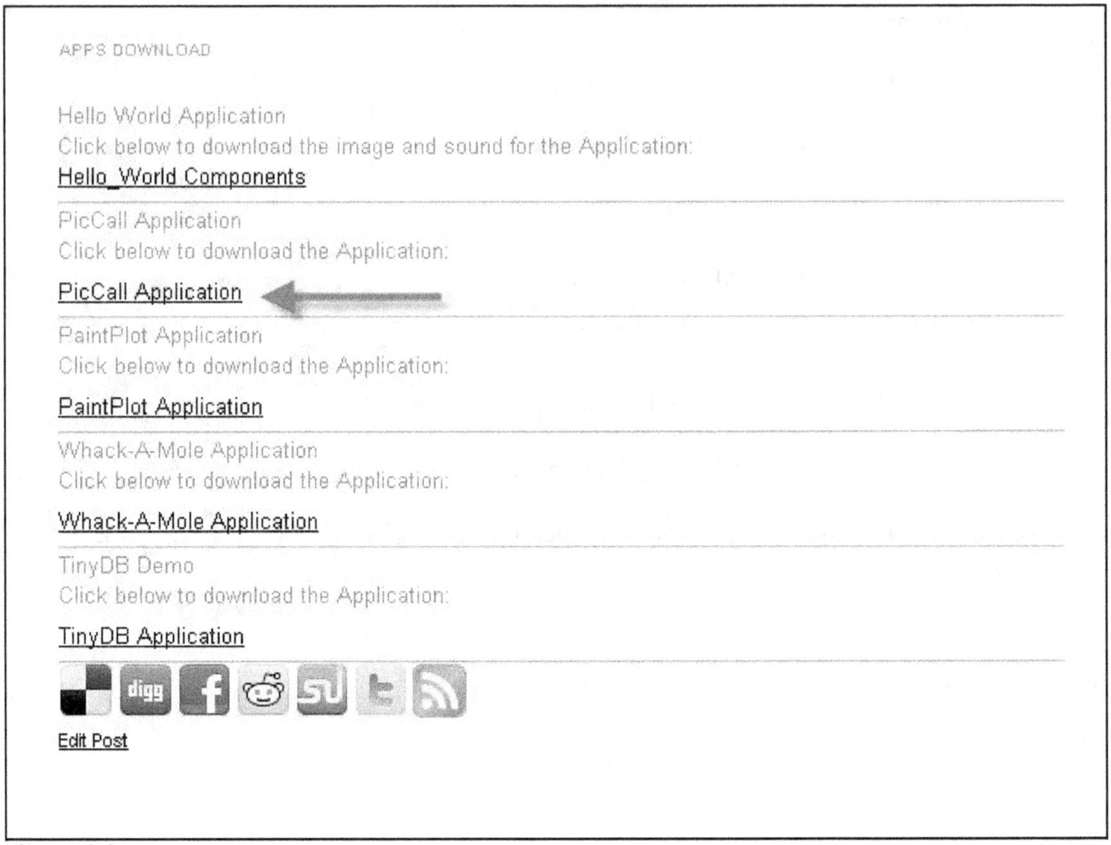

APPS DOWNLOAD
Hello World Application
Click below to download the image and sound for the Application:
Hello_World Components
PicCall Application
Click below to download the Application:
PicCall Application
PaintPlot Application
Click below to download the Application:
PaintPlot Application
Whack-A-Mole Application
Click below to download the Application:
Whack-A-Mole Application
TinyDB Demo
Click below to download the Application:
TinyDB Application
digg
Edit Post

Figure 9.2

Once the PicCall.apk (source file) has been downloaded, we need to upload it to App Inventor.

Inside of "My Projects" click "More Actions". See Figure 9.3.

App Inventor
BETA
My Projects
Design
Learn
New
Delete
More Actions
Projects

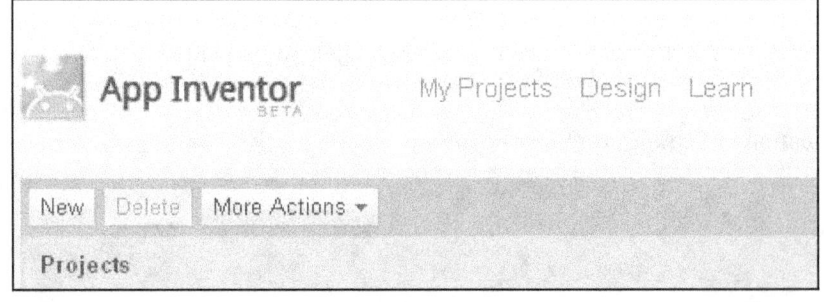

Figure 9.3

Next, click "Upload Source" and select the file called PicCall.zip. See Figure 9.4.

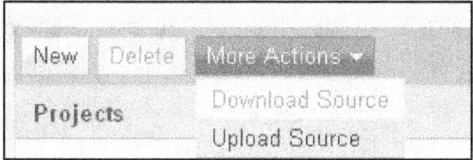

Figure 9.4

Examine the Viewer, Components and Properties. See Figure 9.5.

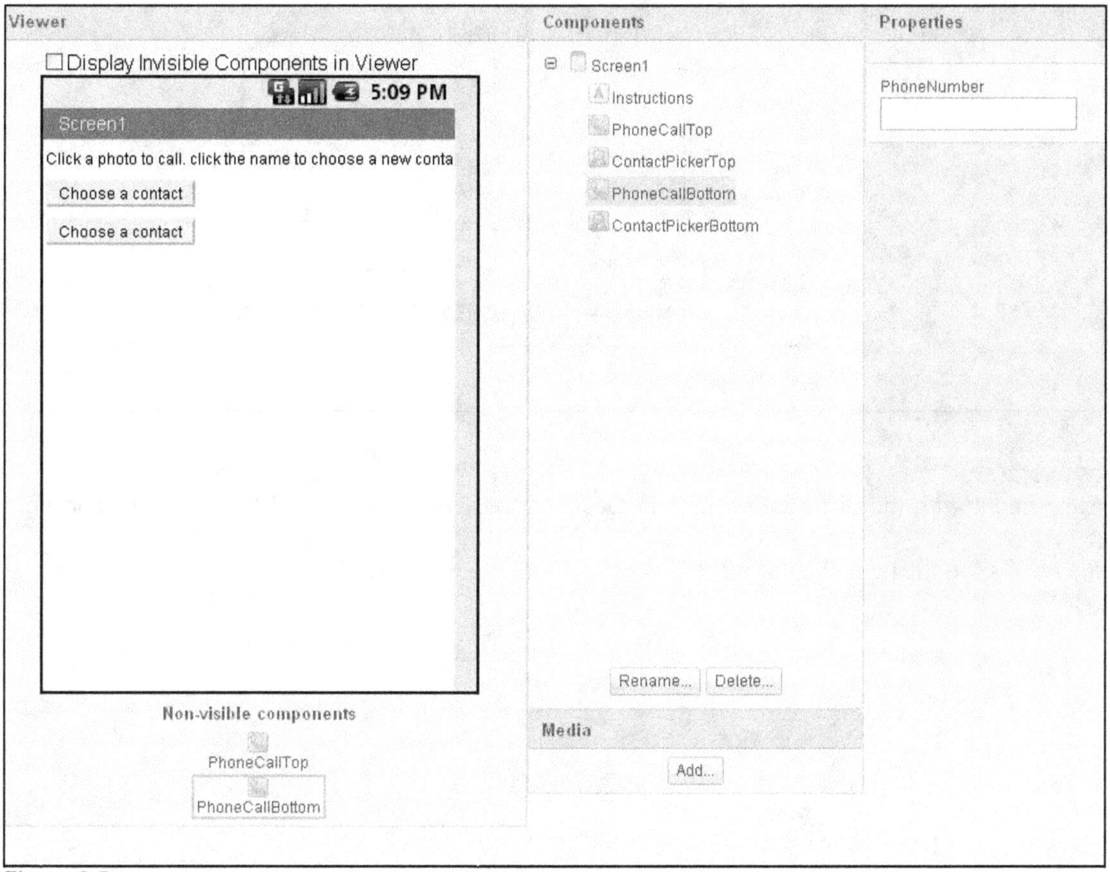

Viewer	Components	Properties
☐ Display Invisible Components in Viewer	⊟ ☐ Screen1	PhoneNumber

Viewer panel:
🔋📶🔋 5:09 PM
Screen1
Click a photo to call. click the name to choose a new conta
Choose a contact
Choose a contact

Non-visible components
PhoneCallTop
PhoneCallBottom

Components panel:
⊟ ☐ Screen1
  Ⓐ Instructions
  PhoneCallTop
  ContactPickerTop
  PhoneCallBottom
  ContactPickerBottom

Rename... Delete...

Media
Add...

Properties panel:
PhoneNumber

Figure 9.5

199

Notice that the Phone Number and other information are missing. This is why nothing happens when we click "Press to Call".

Open the Blocks Editor by clicking "Open Blocks Editor". Notice the configurations. See Figure 9.6.

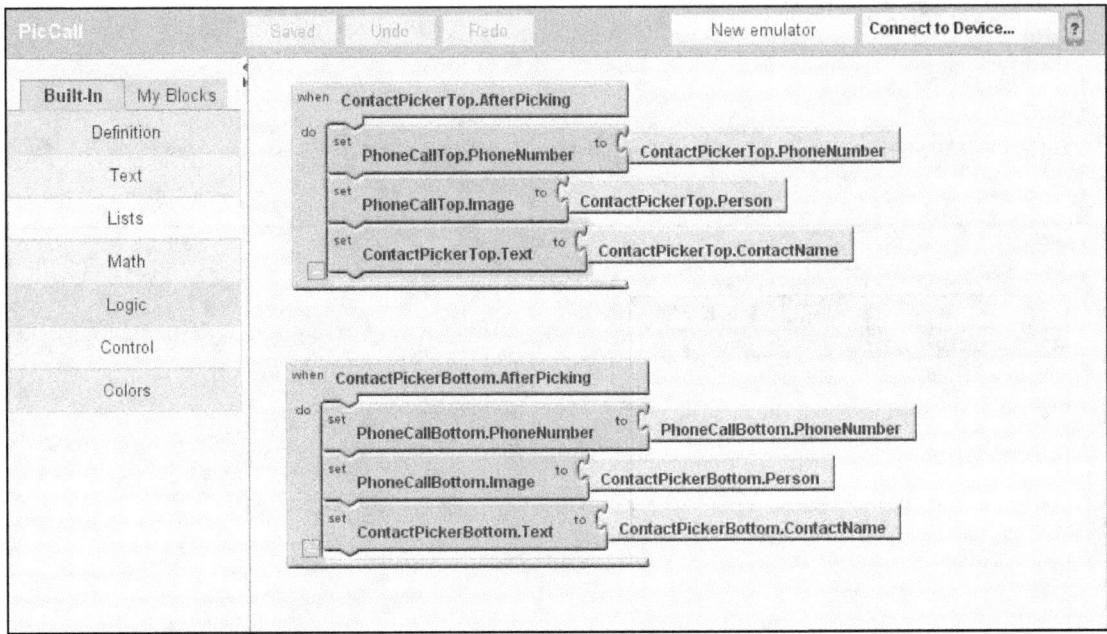

Figure 9.6

Experiment with the different settings in Designer and Blocks Editor. Make changes and note the results. In the next chapter we will continue looking at applications.

10

Your 3rd

Application

"Paint Plot"

PaintPot on Our Device

The PaintPot application is a simple drawing application. We can download the application directly to our device by scanning the QR code. When we do this, we will NOT be able to edit the application.

Scan the QR code. See Figure 10.1.

Figure 10.1

Follow the steps below:

1) Open the QR Droid application on your device.

2) Next, under Decode, click "From camera".

3) Next, line up the scanner with the QR code.

4) Next, the URL for the application will appear.

5) Click "Open" to open the URL.

6) Next, your device will download the application. We will need to install the application.

7) Next, navigate to the location of your applications.

8) Next click Files, click Download then click PaintPot.

9) After installation, open PaintPot.

Use PaintPot to draw some pictures. Experiment with the different buttons and features.

PaintPot in App Inventor

Next, we will download the PaintPot App Inventor source.

Visit the following URL: http://android-apps-development.com/home/apps-download/

Next, click "PaintPot Application" to download it. See Figure 10.2.

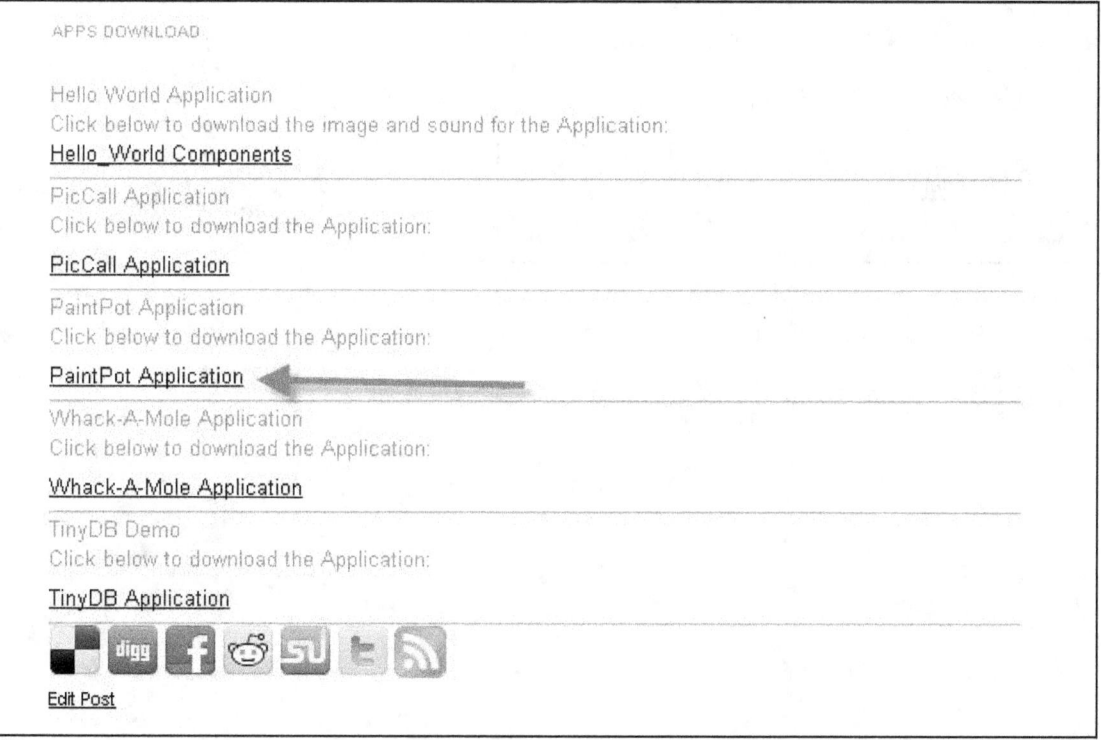

Figure 10.2

Once it has been downloaded, upload it to App Inventor. Inside of "My Projects", click "More Actions" then "Upload Source".

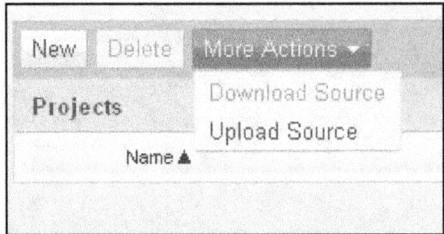

Figure 10.3

Select the file named "PaintPot.zip". See Figure 10.4.

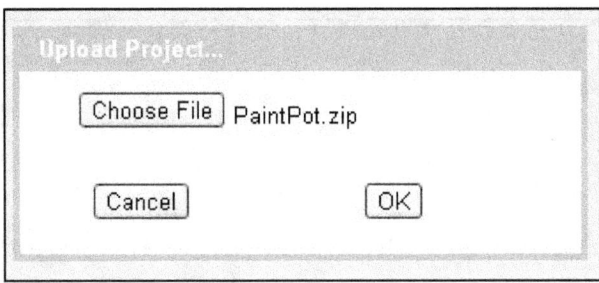

Figure 10.4

Once PaintPot has been uploaded, then review the Viewer, Components and Properties. Experiment and change settings and note the results. See Figure 10.5.

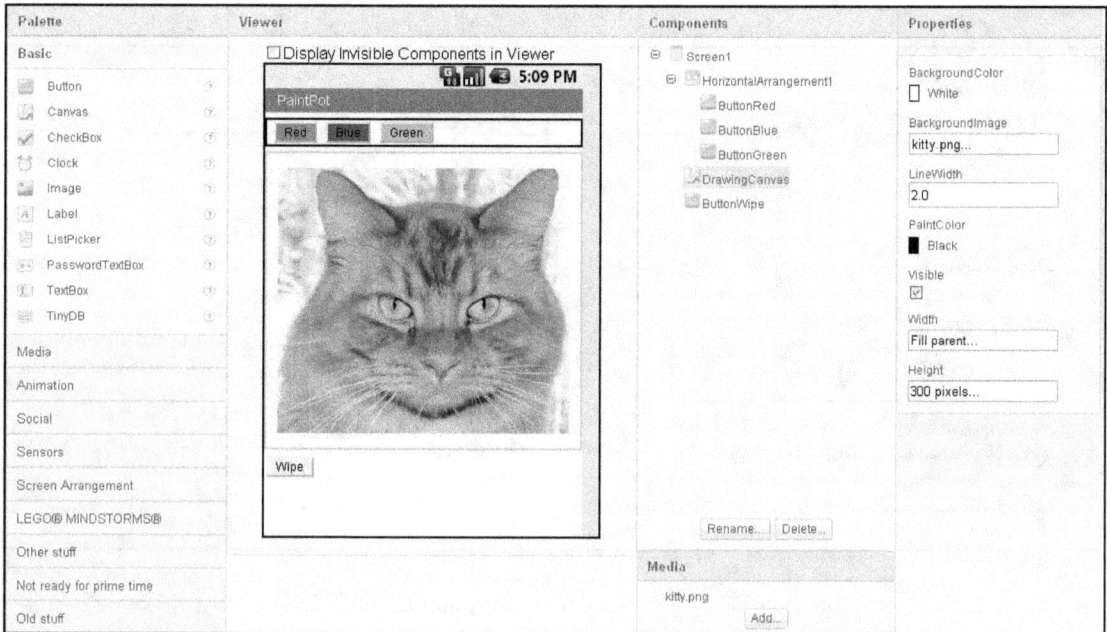

Figure 10.5

205

Open the Blocks Editor and notice the block structure of our application. See Figure 10.6. Notice that all blocks don't have to be connected for our application to function. In an object oriented environment unique events can happen independent of another action. Next, you should experience and change parts of the blocks. Remove sections and note the results.

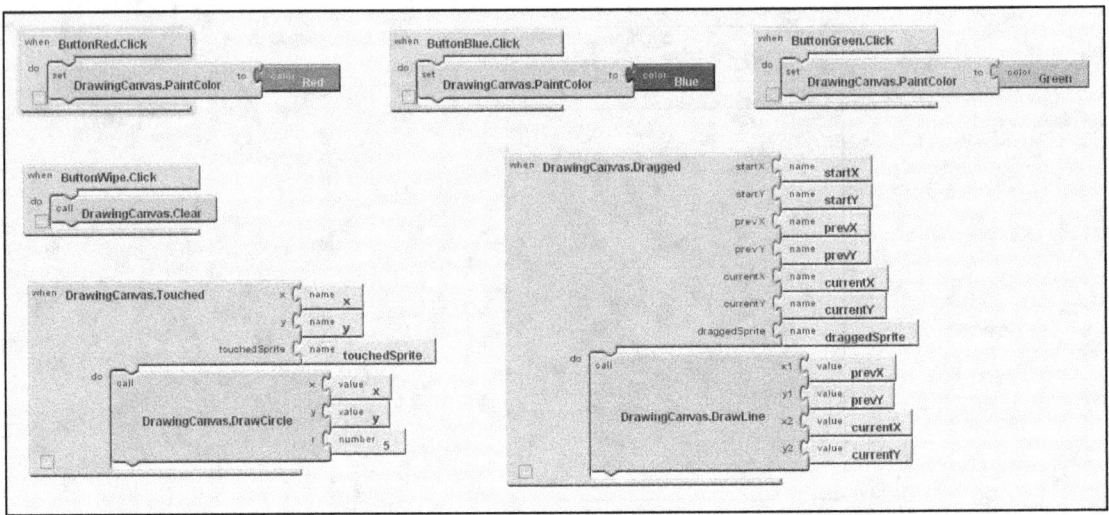

Figure 10.6

In the PaintPot application, we used some new features. In the next chapter we will see additional features in action.

11

Your 4th Application "Tiny DB Demo"

Databases

Before we get into TinyDB, let's talk about databases in general. A database is simply a storage place for information. A database typically consists of fields which hold the actual data. Examples of fields would be name, age or zip code. A record is composed of many fields. An example of a record would be a person. A table in a database stores records.

TinyDB

TinyDB is App Inventor's scaled down version of a database. If you are a database expert, then you will find TinyDB's functionality to be very limited. Nonetheless, TinyDB is very useful for storing information for you application.

TinyDB Application

I used to attend wine tasting events monthly. At each wine tasting event I would sample at least six different wines. In addition, I would try a new wine weekly at various after work business events. So, in a given year, I would sample 120 different wines. What if you wanted to build an application that allowed people to track and rate the wines that they sampled? TinyDB allows you to store information (such as the wine name and your opinion of that wine) which can be retrieved later.

TinyDB Tutorial on Our Device

We can download the TinyDB Tutorial application directly to our device by scanning the QR code. When we do this, we will NOT be able to edit the application.

Scan the QR code. See Figure 11.1.

Figure 11.1

Follow the steps below:

1) Open the QR Droid application on your device.

2) Next, under Decode, click "From camera".

3) Next, line up the scanner with the QR code.

4) Next, the URL for the application will appear.

5) Click "Open" to open the URL.

6) Next, your device will download the application. We will need to install the application.

7) Next, navigate to the location of your applications.

8) Next click Files, click Download then click TinyDB Tutorial.

9) After installation, open TinyDB Tutorial.

Use the TinyDB application and add some contacts to the address book. Experiment with the different buttons and features.

TinyDB Demo in App Inventor

Next, we will download the TinyDB Tutorial App Inventor source.

Visit the following URL: http://android-apps-development.com/home/apps-download/

Next, click "TinyDB Tutorial" to download it. See Figure 11.2.

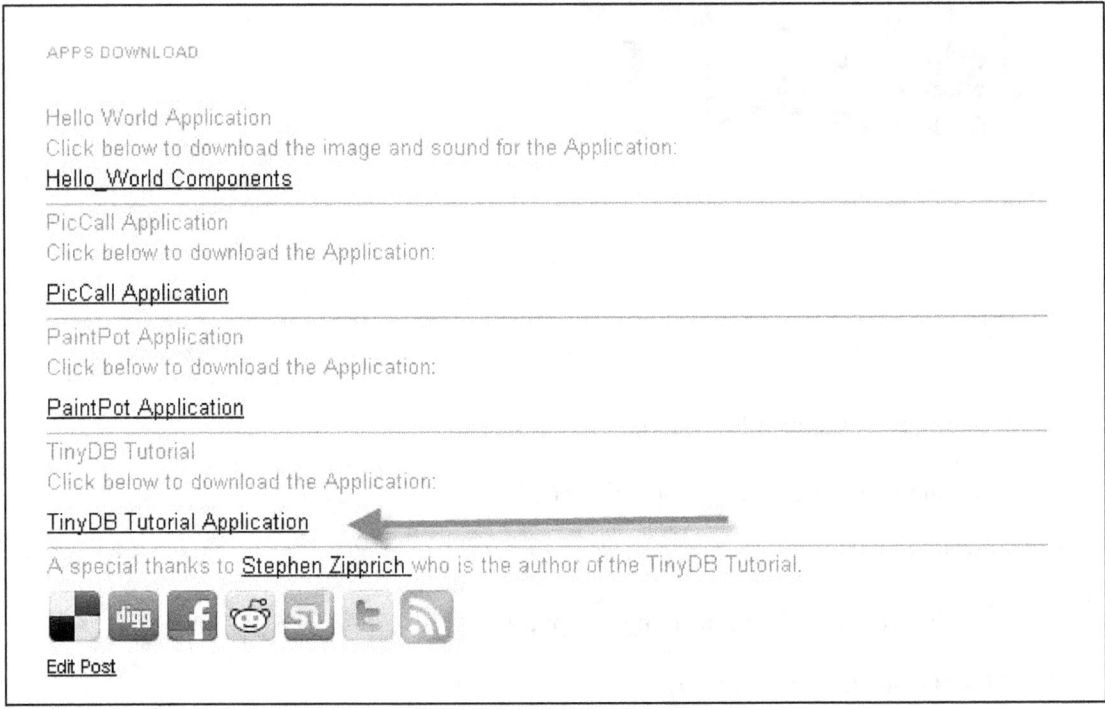

Figure 11.2

In "My Projects", click "More Actions" then click "Upload Source". See Figure 11.3.

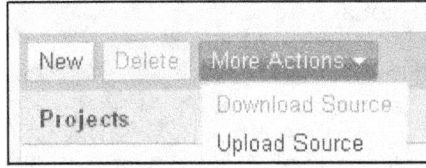

Figure 11.3

Next, choose the zip file named TinyDB_tutorial.zip. See Figure 11.4.

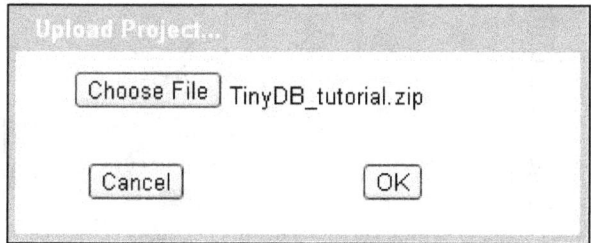

Figure 11.4

The TinyDB Tutorial app has some specific attributes. The following features were setup in Designer. Remember, this is like our list of ingredients for our recipe. Examine the features in Designer. See Figure 11.5.

- 4 Text Boxes

- 1 Label

- 2 Buttons

- 1 Image Component

- 1 Checkbox

- 1 ListPicker

- 3 HorizontalArrangements

- 2 VerticalArrangements

- 1 TinyDB

See Figure 11.5.

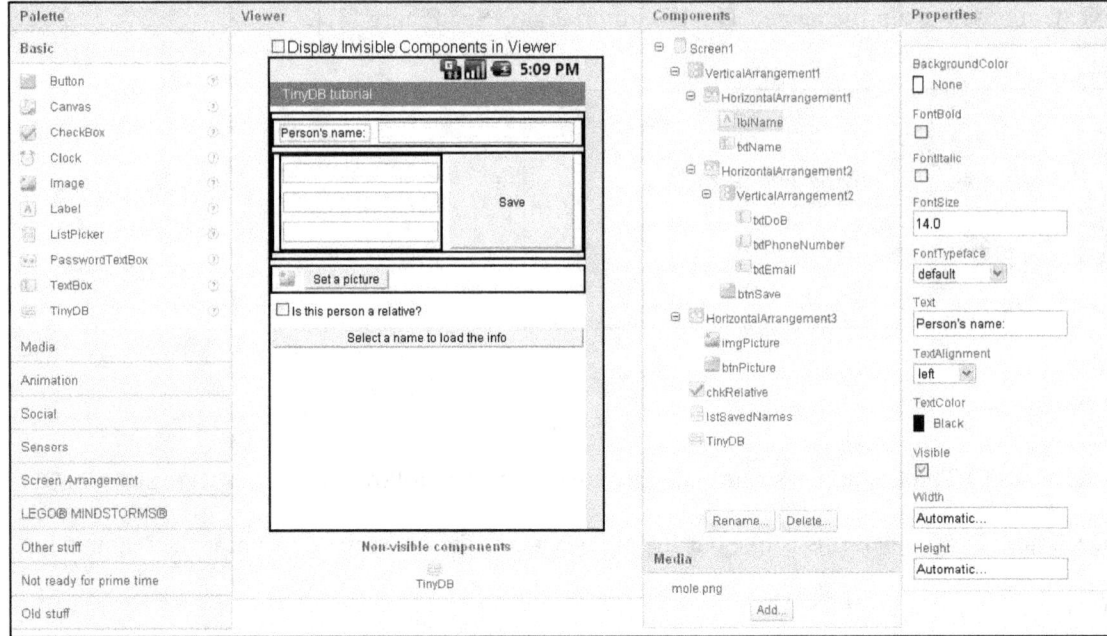

Figure 11.5

Next, we will examine the Blocks Editor. Notice that the Save Button (btnSave.Click) is the backbone of this application. When Save is clicked, all of the actions within that blocked are executed. See Figure 11.6.

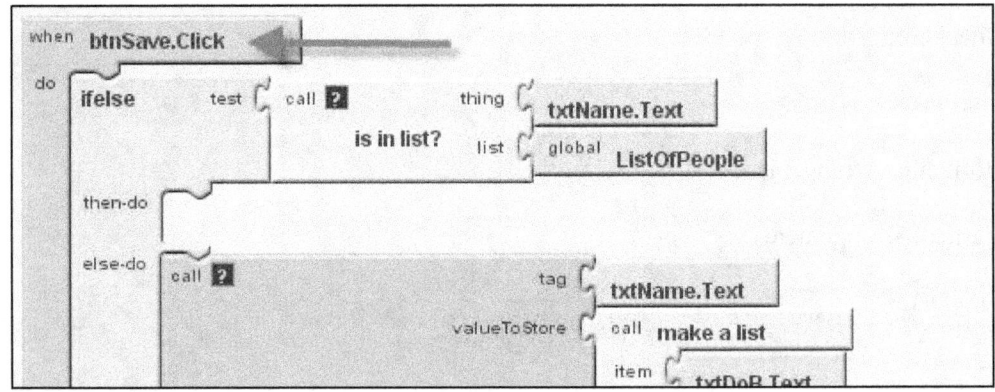

Figure 11.6

212

Notice the "is in list?" block. This ensures that the person that we are adding is not already in the list.

In the next series of blocks, if the entry is not in the list then the information is stored in the TinyDB. See Figure 11.7.

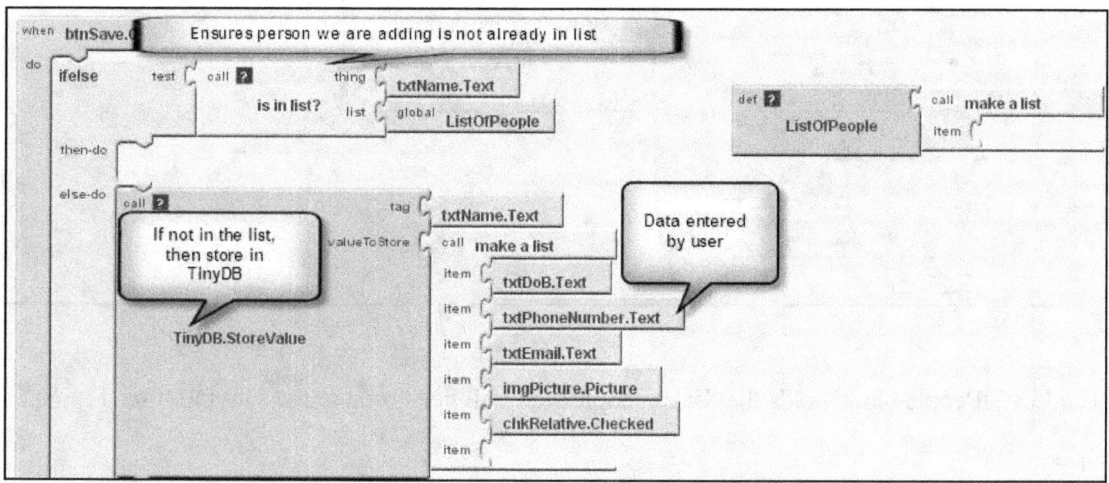

Figure 11.7

The set blocks, in Figure 11.8, reset the input values to allow for new values to be entered.

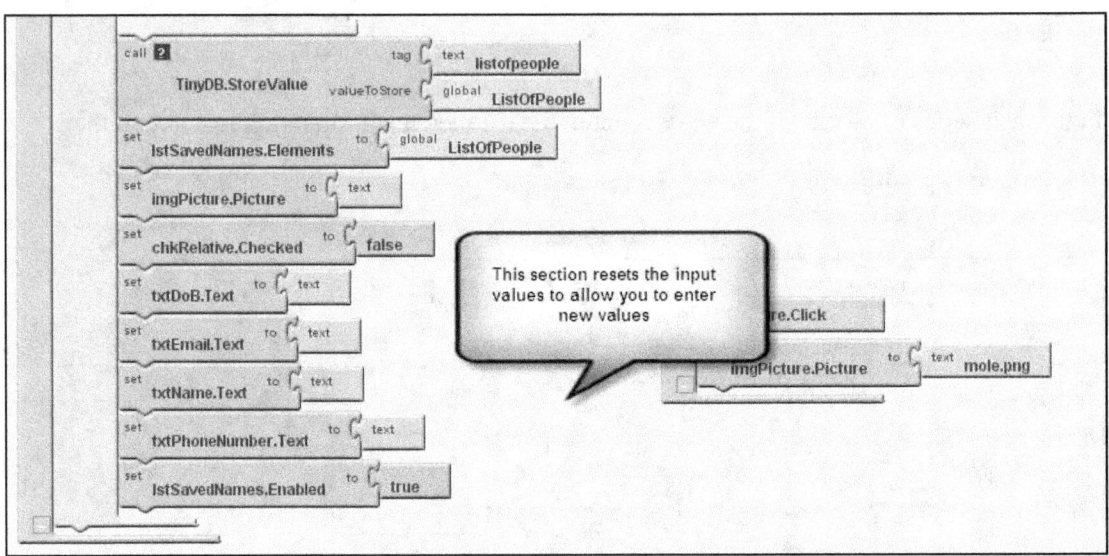

Figure 11.8

The ListOfPeople block holds the list of people who will get stored in the TinyDB. See Figure
11.9.

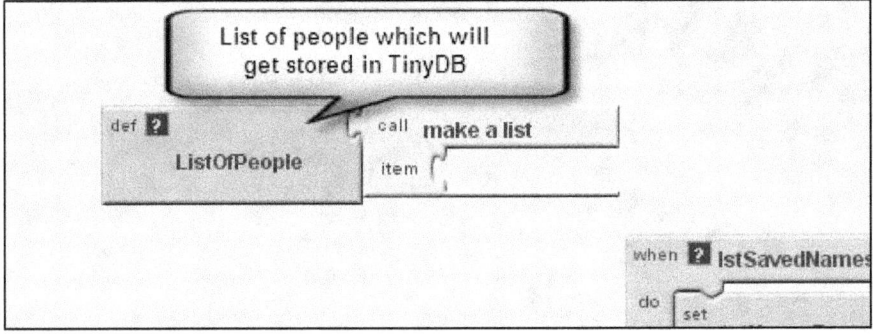

Figure 11.9

The btnPicture.Click block allows the mole image to be shown when the selection is clicked.
See Figure 11.10.

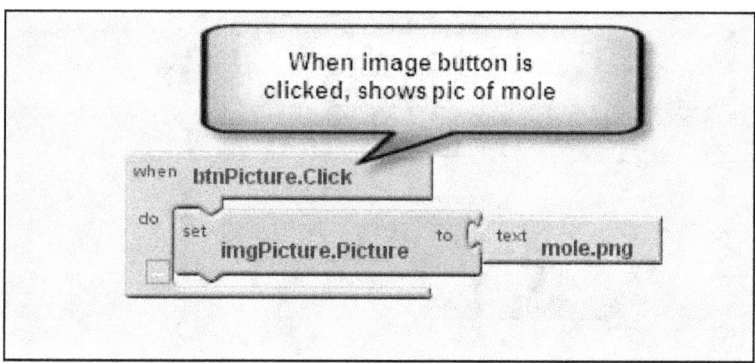

Figure 11.10

The blocks in 11.11 show retrievals from the TinyDB. Notice the blocks titled "TinyDB.GetValue".

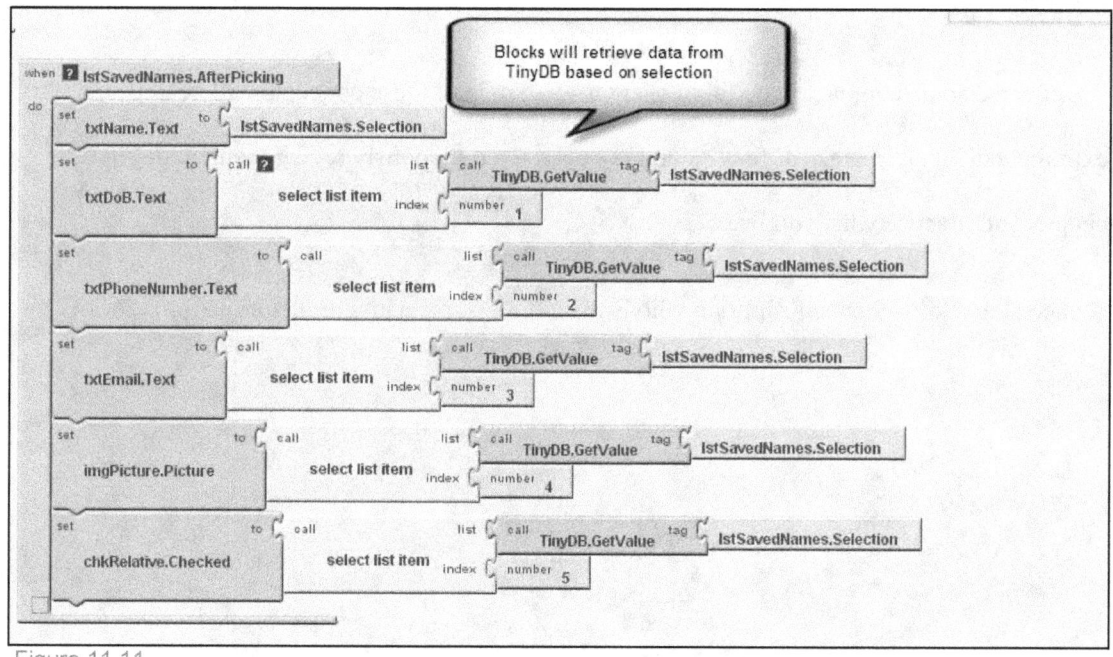

Figure 11.11

During screen initialization, if the TinyDB is empty (or if it does not exist) then do nothing. Else if the TinyDB does exist then load people. If the list is not empty then enable the list picker. See Figure 11.12.

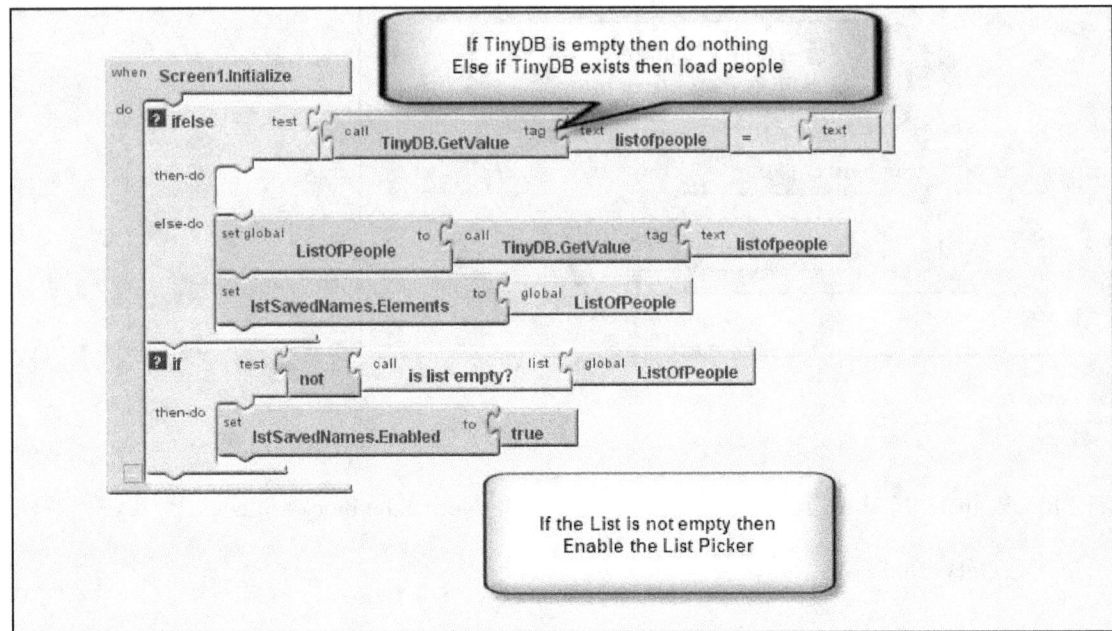

Figure 11.12

We covered some complex material in chapter 11. Some of these concepts will be new and extremely difficult to grasp at first. You may want to continuously revisit the material in this chapter and practice what you learn.

A special thanks to Stephen Zipprich who is the author of the TinyDB Tutorial App. [12]

Source Code and Packaging Your Applications

App Inventor allows you to download the source code of your applications. Your source code

will be in a zip file after downloading. See Figure 11.13.

Figure 11.13

App Inventor allows you to package your application for use on mobile devices. The .apk format

is the format that you have been seeing when you scan the QR codes. You can package your

application into .apk format by clicking "Download to this Computer" from the "Package for

Phone" menu. A .apk file cannot be modified. See Figure 11.14.

Figure 11.14

Android Market

As you may know, Android Market is the place where Android apps are bought and sold. Currently, App Inventor Applications are not allowed on Android Market. The goal for App Inventor is not to build enterprise ready applications for the market, but to give you a learning platform to practice your skills.

In this publication, we covered many aspects of App Inventor. I hope that you have enjoyed this publication and the App Inventor platform. Please provide feedback by visiting http://android-apps-development.com/contacts/ .

12

References

References

1. Google Labs FAQ
   http://www.googlelabs.com/faq.html

2. App Inventor for Android On the Shoulders of Giants

   http://appinventor.googlelabs.com/about/

3. Abacus

   http://en.wikipedia.org/wiki/Abacus

4. Analytical Machine
   http://en.wikipedia.org/wiki/Analytical_Engine

5. Assembly Language
   http://en.wikipedia.org/wiki/Assembly_language

6. von Neumann Architecture
   http://en.wikipedia.org/wiki/Von_Neumann_architecture

7. Computer Programming
   http://en.wikipedia.org/wiki/Computer_programming

8. Mobile Application Development
   http://en.wikipedia.org/wiki/Mobile_application_development

9. Sprite
   http://en.wikipedia.org/wiki/Sprite_%28computer_graphics%29

10. LEGO® MINDSTORMS®
    http://en.wikipedia.org/wiki/Lego_mindstorm

11. QR Codes
    http://en.wikipedia.org/wiki/QR_Code

12. Stephen Zipprich
    http://en.wikipedia.org/wiki/Assembly_language

www.ingramcontent.com/pod-product-compliance
Lightning Source LLC
Chambersburg PA
CBHW081114170526
45165CB00008B/2446